huáng yán péi zhí yè jiào yù sī xiǎng jiǎn dú

黄炎培职业教育思想简读

A Brief Introduction to HuangYanpei's Thoughts on Vocational Education

汉英对照

zhǔ biān chén qióng liú chūn huá
主 编 陈 琼 刘春华

fù zhǔ biān xiān lì lì chén zhēn píng
副主编 先丽莉 陈珍平

cān biān jù yíng lì gū yǒng guì huáng yī mǎ xú wén xuān
参 编 瞿迎利 辜永贵 黄一马 徐文瑄

zhǔ shěn zhāng yáng qún
主 审 张扬群

fān yì xiān lì lì zhōu hǎi xiá zhāng yù liàng
翻 译 先丽莉 周海霞 张玉亮

ChiefEditors ChenQiong LiuChunhua

Associate EditorsXian LiliChen Zhenping

Contributors JuYingli GuYonggui HuangYima XuWenxuan

Chiefreviewer ZhangYangqun

Translators XianLili ZhouHaixia ZhangYuliang

合肥工業大學出版社
HEFEI UNIVERSITY OF TECHNOLOGY PRESS

图书在版编目(CIP)数据

黄炎培职业教育思想简读：汉英对照/陈琼，刘春华主编；先丽莉，周海霞，张玉亮译.--合肥:合肥工业大学出版社，2024.
ISBN 978-7-5650-6861-4

Ⅰ.G40-092.72

中国国家版本馆CIP数据核字第2024XR5707号

黄炎培职业教育思想简读：汉英对照

HUANGYANPEI ZHIYE JIAOYU SIXIANG JIANDU：HANYING DUIZHAO

陈　琼　刘春华　主编　　　先丽莉　周海霞　张玉亮　译

责任编辑　毕光跃
出　　版　合肥工业大学出版社
地　　址　（230009）合肥市屯溪路193号
网　　址　press.hfut.edu.cn
电　　话　理工图书出版中心：0551-62903204
　　　　　营销与储运管理中心：0551-62903198
开　　本　880毫米×1230毫米　1/32
印　　张　5.875
字　　数　160千字
版　　次　2024年9月第1版
印　　次　2024年9月第1次印刷
印　　刷　安徽联众印刷有限公司
发　　行　全国新华书店
书　　号　ISBN 978-7-5650-6861-4
定　　价　28.00元

前言 Preface

黄炎培（1878年10月1日—1965年12月21日）先生是中华职业教育社（1917）创办者，现代职业教育开拓者和中国现代职业教育思想奠基者。

中华职业学校是黄炎培先生于1918年在上海创办的中国近代教育史上第一所专门从事职业教育并以此冠名的学校。抗战期间，学校迁至陪都重庆，为区别于留守上海的中华职业学校，改称中华职业学校渝校。中华职业学校在渝期间坚持办学，为国家培养了大量的专业技术人才，一时成为全国职业教育的典范。

本书主要包括黄炎培职业教育思想简介、黄炎培职业教育论选粹、黄炎培职业教育实践。

本书为中英双语的简明读本，围绕服务国际产能合作和促进职业教育的国际交流与合作的现实需求，选取了黄炎培职业教育论中的精华片段，并用言简意赅的方式解读，力求使读者深入浅出地理解黄炎培职业教育思想的深刻内涵。

本书主要面向“一带一路”沿线国家及海内外“鲁班工坊”的师生群体。通过阅读本书，读者能够了解中国近现代职业教育的发展与成就，能够深入学习黄炎培先生的职业教育思想，并将其应用到自己的教学实践中。此外，由于本书采用中英双语的形式，读者还可以通过中英对照来提高自己的中文水平。同时，本书也适合作为国内职业院校教师的参考用书，帮助教师更好地遵循职业教育教学原则，科学地选择职业教育培养模式和树立质量规格。

读史明智，鉴往知来。作为中国近现代职业教育的先行者，黄炎培职业教育思想具有平民化、实用化、科学化和社会化的特征，不仅开创和推进了中国的职业教育事业，丰富了中国的教育理论，对中国20世纪20—30年代的教育产生了巨大影响，而且以其“大职业教育思想”为代表的思想体系至今对职业教育的研究和发展仍有着积极的指导和推动作用。

前　言

本书由重庆市渝北职业教育中心陈琼、刘春华任主编，先丽莉、陈珍平任副主编，由张扬群担任主审，马庆发[华东师范大学教育学部（原教育科学学院）]任顾问，先丽莉（重庆市渝北职业教育中心）、周海霞（宁波市北仑职业高级中学）、张玉亮（山东科技大学）任翻译，参与编写的还有重庆市渝北职业教育中心瞿迎利、辜永贵、黄一马，江苏中教科信息技术有限公司徐文瑄。本书在编写过程中，得到了重庆市中华职业教育社和中华职业教育社社史陈列馆的大力支持与帮助，并参考了有关著作和研究成果，因篇幅有限，未能一一注明出处，谨向原作者表示衷心感谢。

由于编者水平有限，加上时间仓促，疏漏和不妥之处，敬请专家和读者批评指正。

编　者

2024年3月

qián yán

前言 Preface

Huang Yanpei (October 1, 1878 – December 21, 1965) was the founder of the China Vocational Education Association (1917), a pioneer of modern vocational education, and a founding father of modern Chinese vocational education thought.

In 1918, Mr. Huang founded the Zhonghua Vocational School in Shanghai, the first school in modern Chinese education history to specialize in vocational education and be named as such. During the War of Resistance Against Japan, the school was relocated to Chongqing, the wartime capital, and renamed the Zhonghua Vocational School (Chongqing Campus) to distinguish it from the original school that remained in Shanghai. The Zhonghua Vocational School (Chongqing Campus) persisted in its mission during this period, cultivating a large number of skilled professionals for the nation and becoming a model for vocational education across the country.

This book mainly comprises a brief introduction to Huang Yanpei's thoughts on vocational education, selected excerpts from his works on vocational education, and his practices in vocational education.

As a concise bilingual course book in both Chinese and English, this book focuses on the practical needs of serving international capacity cooperation and promoting international exchange and cooperation in vocational education. It selects the essence of Huang's thoughts on vocational education and provides succinct interpretations, aiming to help readers understand the profound implications of his thoughts in an accessible way.

This book is primarily targeted at teachers and students in countries along the "Belt and Road" and those involved in the Luban Workshop program both domestically and internationally. By reading this book, readers can acquire an understanding of the development and achievements of modern vocational education in China, delve into Huang's thoughts on vocational education, and apply them to their own teaching practices. Additionally, the bilingual format allows readers to enhance their Chinese language proficiency by comparing the Chinese and English texts. Furthermore, this book is suitable as a reference for vocational school teachers in China, assisting them in adhering to the principles of vocational education, scientifically selecting training models, and establishing quality standards.

As we all know, studying history offers wisdom for the future. As a pioneer of modern vocational education in China, Huang's thoughts on vocational education are characterized by their practicality, scientific approach, social orientation, and accessibility to common people. His thoughts not only initiated and promoted vocational education in China, enriched Chinese educational theory, and significantly impacted education in the 1920s and 1930s, but also, as represented by his "Grand Vocational Education Thought", continue to provide active guidance and impetus for the research and development of vocational education today.

This book is edited by Chen Qiong and Liu Chunhua from Chongqing Yubei Vocational Education Center. Xian Lili and Chen Zhenping serve as associate editors, with Zhang Yangqun as the chief reviewer and Ma Qingfa [Facullty of Education (Original School of Education Science), East China Normal University] as the consultant. The translation is carried out by Xian Lili (Chongqing Yubei Vocational Education Center), Zhou Haixia (Ningbo Beilun Vocational School), and Zhang Yuliang (Shandong University of Science and Technology). Other contributors include Qu Yingli, Gu Yonggui, and Huang Yima from Chongqing Yubei Vocational Education Center, as well as Xu Wenxuan from CNEDUTECH. During the compilation of this book, we received generous support and assistance from the China Vocational Education Association (CVEA) and its History Exhibition Hall. We also referred to relevant works and research findings. Due to space limitations, we were unable to individually cite all sources. We extend our sincere gratitude to the original authors for their invaluable contributions.

Due to the limitations of the editors and the tight timeline, there may be inadvertent omissions or errors in this book. We sincerely welcome feedback and corrections from experts and readers.

Editors
March 2024

目录 Contents

第一篇 Part 1

黄炎培职业教育思想简介

A Brief Introduction to Huang's Thoughts on Vocational Education

黄炎培（1878年10月1日—1965年12月21日），号楚南，字任之，笔名抱一，出生于川沙镇内史第，江苏省川沙县（今上海市）人。黄炎培先生长期致力于教育救国事业。早在1898年任私塾教师，1901年考入南洋公学，1903年因其所在的班级闹学潮而被解散后，他立志走教育救国的道路，回到家乡先后创办川沙小学和川沙中学。辛亥革命后，担任江苏省教育司司长，致力于推动江苏省的教育改革和发展。1917年5月6日，他在上海联络教育界和实业界人士，发起成立了中华职业教育社，由此，他带领中华职教社同仁研究和倡导职业教育，全力推动职业教育在中

guó de fā zhǎn
国的发展。

huáng xiān sheng zài cháng qī de jiào yù gōng zuò zhōng　　duì zhōng guó chuán tǒng jiào yù de gǎi gé
黄先生在长期的教育工作中，对中国传统教育的改革、

zhí yè jiào yù de yán jiū hé shí shī　　zuò chū le zhuó yuè gòng xiàn　　wèi wǒ men liú xià le
职业教育的研究和实施，做出了卓越贡献，为我们留下了

bǎo guì de jīng shén cái fù　　huáng yán péi xiān sheng de zhí yè jiào yù sī xiǎng hé jiào yù shí jiàn
宝贵的精神财富。黄炎培先生的职业教育思想和教育实践

jīng yàn　　duì wǒ men jīn tiān shēn huà jiào yù gǎi gé　　fā zhǎn hé bàn hǎo zhí yè jiào yù
经验，对我们今天深化教育改革、发展和办好职业教育，

jù yǒu jiè jiàn yì yì hé shí dài jià zhí　　wèi cǐ　　wǒ men duì tā zhí yè jiào yù jiào yù
具有借鉴意义和时代价值。为此，我们对他职业教育教育

sī xiǎng hé jiào yù shí jiàn jīng yàn de jī běn tè diǎn　　guī nà yǐ xià jǐ diǎn rèn shi　　gòng
思想和教育实践经验的基本特点，归纳以下几点认识，供

dú zhě cān kǎo
读者参考。

Huang Yanpei（October 1, 1878 — December 21, 1965）, also known
as Chunan, with the courtesy name Renzhi and pen name Baoyi, was born
in a distinguished family in Chuansha Town, Jiangsu Province（now
Shanghai）. He dedicated his life to the cause of education for national
salvation. As early as 1898, he worked as a private school teacher. In 1901,
he was admitted to Nanyang Public School. In 1903, after his class was
disbanded due to student protests, he resolved to pursue education as a
means to save the nation.Returning to his hometown, he founded Chuansha
Primary School and Chuansha Middle School. After the Revolution of
1911, he served as the director of the Jiangsu Provincial Department of
Education, devoting himself to promoting educational reform and
development in the province. On May 6, 1917, he joined hands with
important figures from the education and industrial sectors and initiated

the establishment of the China Vocational Education Association (CVEA) in Shanghai. He led the association in researching and advocating for vocational education , wholeheartedly promoting its development in China.

Throughout his long career in education , Huang made remarkable contributions to the reform of traditional Chinese education and the research and implementation of vocational education , leaving behind a precious spiritual legacy. His educational philosophy and practical experience in vocational education hold valuable lessons and contemporary significance for us today as we deepen educational reforms , develop and improve vocational education. To this end , we have summarized the following key points regarding his vocational education philosophy and practical experience for readers' reference.

1. 爱国主义和人道主义是基础 Patriotism and Humanitarianism as the Foundation

ài guó zhǔ yì hé rén dào zhǔ yì shì jī chǔ

ài guó zhǔ yì hé rén dào zhǔ yì shì huáng yán péi jiào yù sī xiǎng 、 jiào yù shí jiàn jīng yàn
爱国主义和人道主义是黄炎培教育思想、教育实践经验

xíng chéng hé fā zhǎn de jī chǔ
形成和发展的基础。

Patriotism and humanitarianism formed the foundation of Huang's educational thought and practice.

huáng yán péi xiān sheng chéng zhǎng yú guó jiā bīn yú wēi wáng 、 rén mín kǔ nàn shēn zhòng de nián
黄炎培先生成长于国家濒于危亡、人民苦难深重的年

dài lǐ , zǎo nián jiù huái yǒu shēn qiè de ài guó rè qíng , yǐ jiù guó jiù mín wéi jǐ rèn
代里,早年就怀有深切的爱国热情,以救国救民为己任。

他考入南洋公学后，师承蔡元培，全力响应蔡元培的教育救国主张，立志献身于教育事业。经过调研考察，他痛感当时兴办的学堂完全脱离社会经济和平民生计，弊端严重，“殊与救国之道相背驰”。为此，他认定“提倡爱国之本在于职业教育”，并明确指出：“凡职业教育宜以经济为中心，而以教育为其手段可也。”

Huang grew up in an era when the nation was on the verge of collapse and the people were suffering deeply. From a young age, he harbored a profound patriotic passion and took it upon himself to save the country and its people. After entering Nanyang Public School, he studied under Cai Yuanpei and wholeheartedly responded to Cai's advocacy for education as a means of national salvation, vowing to dedicate himself to the cause of education. Through research and investigation, he lamented that the schools established at the time were completely detached from the social economy and the livelihoods of ordinary people, with serious drawbacks that "ran counter to the path of national salvation". Therefore, he firmly believed that "promoting patriotism lies in vocational education" and clearly stated that "all vocational education should be centered on the economy, with education as the means".

黄炎培先生的爱国主义是与人道主义融合在一起的。他的人道主义主要来源于“民，吾同胞；物，吾与也”的儒家思想。他认为：“求生”和“求群”是人类的根本需要。求生必须具有适合于生存和发展的知能，求群就要有爱群、爱家、爱国的情感。教育、职业教育的宗旨就是使人“广其知而大其爱”。为了尊重人道，强调：“办职业教育，须下决心为大多数平民谋幸福。”

Huang's patriotism was intertwined with humanitarianism. His humanitarianism primarily originated from the Confucian thought of "all people are my brothers and sisters, and all living things are my companions". He believed that the fundamental needs of humanity are "survival" and "community". Survival requires knowledge and skills suitable for existence and development, while community necessitates love for the group, family, and country. The purpose of education, especially vocational education, is to enable people to "broaden their knowledge and deepen their love". To respect humanity, he emphasized: "In developing vocational education, we must be determined to seek happiness for the majority of ordinary people".

毋庸置疑，真诚的爱国主义和人道主义者，在反对帝国主义、封建主义和法西斯主义的革命斗争中，从而转变成为社会主义的拥戴者，而黄先生则是其中具有代表性的杰出人物之一。

Undoubtedly, sincere patriots and humanitarians transformed into supporters of socialism during the revolutionary struggles against imperialism, feudalism, and fascism, and Huang was one of the outstanding representatives among them.

第一次世界大战（1914—1918年）期间，欧美强国暂时放松了对我国的侵略，我国民族工商业有了复苏与发展的机会。在当时形势下，黄先生秉持着爱国主义和人道主义的信念，一心致力于职教事业来振兴国家经济，改善人民生计。1917年，黄先生在由他起草的《中华职业教育社宣言书》中，阐明了职业教育的功能，希望十年而后，实现“学校无不用之成材，社会无不学之执业，国无不教之民，民无不乐之生……”的理想。然而，经历半殖民地半封建社会的旧中国的长期磨炼和反复教训，到1926年，他感慨地说：“我们同志八九年来所做工作……也算尽心力而为之了。可是我们所希望，百分之七八十没有达到。”他看清了之所以没有达到的原因主要在于“国事捣乱”和“社会经济困难”。于是，坚持以救国救民为己任的黄先生提出“大职业教育主义”，要求“办职业学校的，须同时和一切教育界、职业界努力沟通联络；提倡职业教育的，同时须分一部分精神，参加全社会的运动”。他还要求努力使职业教育为更广大的平民大众服务，除在城市开办各种形式的职业学校和职业补习学校等外、积极开展“富教结合”的农村改进实验区的工作。这说明，随着时势的变化、他对职业教育与国家社会乃至世界全局的关系有了新的认识。1931年九一八事变的爆发，促使黄先生的这种认识进一步深化。随着抗日民族统一战线的广泛建立，黄先生集中精力参加抗日救国运动。他的教育思想和职业教育活动有了新的发展。中华职业教育社的工作进入“努力使职业教育以配合国家民族为中心”的新时期。

During World War I (1914 – 1918), as the major powers of Europe and America temporarily eased their aggression towards China, China's national industry and commerce experienced a resurgence and development. In this context, driven by his patriotic and humanitarian beliefs, Huang devoted himself to the cause of vocational education to revitalize the national economy and improve people's livelihoods. In 1917, in *the Declaration of the China Vocational Education Association*, which he drafted, Huang elucidated the functions of vocational education, envisioning a future where "in every school, each individual can be nurtured to be useful; in society, every profession requires continuous learning, thus the nation has no uneducated citizens, and all the people live a happy life..." However, after enduring the trials and tribulations of semi-colonial and semi-feudal old China, by 1926, he lamented: "The work we have done in the past eight or nine years... can be considered as having been done with all our heart. But what we hoped for, seventy to eighty percent has not been achieved." He realized that the main reasons for this lack of achievement were "national turmoil" and "socioeconomic difficulties." Therefore, Huang, who persisted in his mission to save the country and its people, proposed the "Grand Vocational Education" initiative, advocating that "those who run vocational schools must simultaneously strive to communicate and connect with all educational and vocational circles; those who promote vocational education must also devote a portion of their energy to participate in the movements of the whole society". He also urged efforts to make vocational education serve a wider range of ordinary people, not only by establishing various forms of vocational schools and supplementary schools in cities but also by actively developing "combining education with wealth creation" in rural experimental areas. This illustrates that with the changing times, he gained new insights into the relationship between vocational education and the nation, society, and even the global situation. The outbreak of the September 18th Incident in 1931 further deepened Huang's understanding. With the establishment of a broad Chinese United Front against

Japanese Aggression, Huang concentrated his energy on participating in the anti– Japanese invasion and national salvation movement. His educational thoughts and vocational education activities entered a new phase. The work of the CVEA entered a new era of “striving to align vocational education with national needs”.

抗日战争开始后，黄先生响应中国共产党提出的建立“抗日民族统一战线”的号召，与中华职业教育社的同志们积极参加民主抗战运动，明确宣告：职业教育的目标，“往远处说，是在实现一个民生幸福的社会，在那社会里，确切达到了“无业者有业、有业者乐业”的目的。……就近处说，本社的使命是在以最高的积极性，参与抗战建国的努力。吾们确信，职业教育，只有在民族解放、民权平等、民生幸福的社会里，才能实现其造福人群的理想”。1945年抗日战争胜利后，黄先生坚持民主进步的立场，站在中国共产党领导的人民解放运动的一边，为夺取人民解放斗争的胜利而奋斗。同时他十分重视对战后教育问题的研究，强调“在战争结束以后，需要生产的恢复和增益”，更要提高对职业教育的认识和估价。

After the War of Resistance against Japanese Aggression began, Huang responded to the call of the Communist Party of China to establish a "Chinese United Front against Japanese Aggression" and actively participated in the democratic resistance movement with his colleagues from the CVEA. He clearly declared that the goal of vocational education was "ultimately, to create a society where everyone's livelihood is secure and fulfilling, where the unemployed find meaningful work and the employed find joy in their work... In the short term, the mission of our association is to participate in the efforts of resisting aggression and building the nation with the highest enthusiasm. We firmly believe that vocational education can only achieve its ideal of benefiting the people in a society with national liberation, equal civil rights, and happy livelihoods". After the victory of the War of Resistance against Japanese Aggression in 1945, Huang maintained his commitment to democracy and progress, aligning himself with the people's liberation movement led by the Chinese Communist Party and contributing to its eventual triumph. At the same time, he attached great importance to the research of post-war education issues, emphasizing that "after the war ends, there is a need for the restoration and increase of production", and even more importantly, to enhance the understanding and appreciation of vocational education.

1949年，新中国成立之初，黄先生发表了《中华职业教育社奋斗三十二年发现的新生命》。对当年"一系列的人受了他们广泛的、天真的人道主义和国家民族主义这些思想的驱使，前前后后奋斗几十年”的曲折前进过程，做了系统的总结。并说明：“开展职业教育，是今后增加生产、繁荣经济的国策实施时所必要采取的措施”，“在今后建国大计的需要上必然地很广大而且很急迫”。同时表明：中华职业教育社一群人积极参加了抗日战争、民主运动和解放战争，“得到了充分的信心来迎接新时代”。由此，黄先生等毕生为之奋斗的中华职业教育社的事业有了新的生命，在今天的新形势下，放出新的光彩。

In 1949, at the beginning of the founding of the People's Republic of China, Huang published *The New Life Discovered in CVEA after 32 Years of Struggle*. He systematically summarized the tortuous progress of "a cohort of individuals driven by their broad" innocent humanitarianism and nationalism, who had persevered for decades". He also explained that "developing vocational education is a necessary measure in implementing the national policy to increase production and prosper the economy", and "it will inevitably be vast and urgent in the needs of future nation-building". At the same time, he stated that the group of people from the CVEA actively participated in the War of Resistance against Japanese Aggression, the democratic movement, and the liberation war, and "have gained full confidence to welcome the new era". Thus, the cause of the CVEA for which Huang and others dedicated their lives, gained new life and shone with new brilliance in today's new situation.

2. 理实结合，身体力行倡导职业教育

Integrating Theory with Practice, Advocating Vocational Education through Actions

黄炎培大力倡导职业教育，对职业教育的理论探讨和实验研究做出了卓越的贡献。

黄先生教育思想和教育实践的一个突出特点，是认定沟通教育与职业教育是当时教育改革的重要关键，高度重视职业教育对增加生产、繁荣经济和解决人民生计问题的重大意义和作用。他研究了美、日等外国的教育学说并考察了各种教育设施，总结我国清末民初兴办所谓新学堂的经验和教训，由提倡实用主义教育转而倡导职业教育。与此同时，他身体力行，先后创办了中华职业学校、职业补习学校和职业指导所等教育实体。在长期的实验研究和理论探讨中，他对职业教育的基本含义、目的和实施方针等重

yào wèn tí　　　fā biǎo le hěn duō hán yǒu zhēn zhī zhuó jiàn de lùn zhù　　zhì jīn réng rán zhí dé
要问题，发表了很多含有真知灼见的论著，至今仍然值得

wǒ men rèn zhēn xué xí
我们认真学习。

Huang was a strong advocate for vocational education and made significant contributions to its theoretical exploration and experimental research.

A prominent feature of Huang's educational philosophy and practice was his belief that bridging the gap between general education and vocational education was key to educational reform at the time. He placed great emphasis on the significance of vocational education in boosting production, stimulating the economy, and improving people's livelihoods. He studied educational theories and practices in countries like the United States and Japan, inspected various educational facilities, and drew lessons from China's experiences in establishing new schools during the late Qing Dynasty and early Republican period. Based on these insights, he shifted his focus from advocating for pragmatic education to championing vocational education. Huang was not just a theorist, but a practitioner as well. He established several educational institutions, including the Zhonghua Vocational School, vocational supplementary schools, and vocational guidance centers. Through years of experimental research and theoretical exploration, he published numerous insightful works on fundamental issues of vocational education, such as its definition, goals, and implementation strategies. These works remain valuable resources for us to study and learn from today.

1）关于职业教育的基本含义

Meaning of Vocational Education

关于职业教育的定义历来有不同的说法。黄先生在不少论著中对职业教育的含义均有提及。首先，他认为职业起源于社会分工，“社会生活方式采用分工制”，于是乎便有了职业和职业教育。他在《职业教育基本理论纲要》等文章中，对职业和职业教育的基本含义作了简要的说明。其次，他认为职业就是“用劳力或劳心换取生活需求的日常工作”，是“一种确定的互助行为”，是“对己谋生，对群服务”。职业教育是依据人们分担的“日常工作”（即职业）的需要，“启发人的知能”，“给人以互助行为的素养”，“使人人广其知而大其爱”，“了解我与群的关系”，贡献他的力量来“换取生活需求”并“对群服务”。再次，黄先生把人们日常的劳动分工和人群之间的互助合作关系联系起来诠释职业的基本含义，把教育和职业结合起来阐述职业教育的基本含义，就职业和职业教育本身看来，是合

hū qíng lǐ de　　　duì wǒ men jīn tiān liǎo jiě hé yán jiū zhí yè jiào yù de běn zhì hé gōng
乎情理的。对我们今天了解和研究职业教育的本质和功

néng　　tí shēng duì zhí yè jiào yù de dì wèi hé zuò yòng de rèn shí shì hěn yǒu qǐ fā de
能，提升对职业教育的地位和作用的认识是很有启发的。

There have always been different interpretations regarding the definition of vocational education. Huang touched upon the meaning of vocational education in many of his works. First, he believed that vocations originated from the division of labor in society, stating that "social life adopts a division of labor system", thus giving rise to vocations and vocational education. In articles such as *Basic Theoretical Outline of Vocational Education*, he provided a concise explanation of the fundamental meaning of vocations and vocational education. In addition, he defined vocation as "daily work that uses physical or mental labor to exchange for life's necessities", a "certain kind of mutual aid behavior", and "earning a living for oneself and serving the community". Vocational education, based on the needs of people's "daily work (vocations)", aims to "inspire people's knowledge and skills", "cultivate people's ability for mutual aid", "enable everyone to broaden their knowledge and deepen their love", "understand the relationship between oneself and the community", and contribute their strength to "exchange for life's necessities" and "serve the community". Furthermore, Huang interpreted the basic meaning of vocations by linking people's daily division of labor with the cooperative relationship between individuals. He also elaborated on the fundamental meaning of vocational education by combining education with vocations. In terms of vocations and vocational education themselves, this is reasonable. It provides valuable inspirations for us today to understand and research the nature and functions of vocational education, and to enhance our recognition of its status and role.

zuì hòu huáng xiān sheng duì zhí yè jiào yù jǐ běn hán yì de lùn shù shì hé dāng nián wǒ guó

最后，黄先生对职业教育基本含义的论述是和当年我国教育的实际问题密切联系的。他的主导思想，就是要沟通教育与职业来改革教育脱离社会生产和人民生活的严重弊端。所以他认为，发展和办好职业教育是沟通教育与职业的重要途径，同时，普通教育也应有与职业沟通的内容。他力求普通教育与职业教育沟通配合起来。要求职业学校在加强职业知识技能培训的同时，也要培育和提高学生多方面的素质，使之成为“社会国家的健全良好分子”。他认为对普通学校，特别是普通中学，其教学内容应该包含有职业教育的内容，采取施行职业指导和在高中阶段设职业科等办法，使不能升学的学生具备切实的知识技能来谋生。他当时的这种要求对我们今天的教育改革也极具现实意义。

jiào yù de shí jì wèn tí mì qiè lián xì de tā de zhǔ dǎo sī xiǎng jiù shì yào gōu tōng

jiào yù yǔ zhí yè lái gǎi gé jiào yù tuō lí shè huì shēng chǎn hé rén mín shēng huó de yán zhòng bì

duān suǒ yǐ tā rèn wéi fā zhǎn hé bàn hǎo zhí yè jiào yù shì gōu tōng jiào yù yǔ zhí yè

de zhòng yào tú jìng tóng shí pǔ tōng jiào yù yě yīng yǒu yǔ zhí yè gōu tōng de nèi róng

tā lì qiú pǔ tōng jiào yù yǔ zhí yè jiào yù gōu tōng pèi hé qǐ lái yào qiú zhí yè xué xiào

zài jiā qiáng zhí yè zhī shi jì néng péi xùn de tóng shí yě yào péi yù hé tí gāo xué shēng duō

fāng miàn de sù zhì shǐ zhī chéng wéi shè huì guó jiā de jiàn quán liáng hǎo fèn zǐ tā rèn

wéi duì pǔ tōng xué xiào tè bié shì pǔ tōng zhōng xué qí jiào xué nèi róng yīng gāi bāo hán yǒu

zhí yè jiào yù de nèi róng cǎi qǔ shī xíng zhí yè zhǐ dǎo hé zài gāo zhōng jiē duàn shè zhí yè

kē děng bàn fǎ shǐ bù néng shēng xué de xué shēng jù bèi qiè shí de zhī shi jì néng lái móu

shēng tā dāng shí de zhè zhǒng yāo qiú duì wǒ men jīn tiān de jiào yù gǎi gé yě jí jù xiàn shí

yì yì

Finally, Huang's discussion of the basic meaning of vocational education was closely linked to the practical issues of education in China at the time. His main idea was to integrate education with vocational training to address the significant disconnect between education and the practical needs of society and the economy. Therefore, he believed that developing and improving vocational education was a crucial way to connect education with vocations. At the same time, general education should also include content related to vocational communications. He strived to integrate general education with vocational education, requiring vocational schools to not only strengthen the training of vocational knowledge and skills but also cultivate and improve students' overall qualities, making them "sound and good members of society and the nation". He believed that general schools, especially secondary schools, should incorporate vocational education content into their curricula, implement career guidance, and offer vocational courses in high school to equip students who cannot pursue higher education with practical knowledge and skills for employment. This demand he made at the time is also highly relevant to our current educational reform.

2）关于职业教育的目的

Goals of Vocational Education

在中华职业教育社第一届年会上，经黄先生提议，确定了职业教育的目的。这就是："为个人谋生之准备，为个人服务社会之准备，为国家及世界增进生产力之准备。"由于有些人认为职业教育只是一种技艺教育，不足以发展个性。所以后来增加“为谋个性之发展”一条，并列为第一个目的。黄先生在《职业教育基本理论纲要》中指出“自社会生活方式采分工制，求工作效能的增进与工作者天性、天才的认识与浚发，进而与其工作适合，于是乎有职业教育”。这里讲的“天性、天才”含有个性的意义。黄先生还曾强调：要“用教育方法，使人人依其个性获得生活的供给和乐趣，同时尽其对群之义务”。这都说明了职业教育与个性发展的密切关系。

At the first annual meeting of the CVEA, Huang proposed and established the goals of vocational education, namely, “equipping individuals with the skills to earn a living, fostering a sense of social responsibility, and contributing to national and global productivity”. Some people believed that vocational education was merely a form of technical training and insufficient for personal development. Therefore, another goal, “promoting individual development”, was later added and listed as the primary goal. In the *Basic Theoretical Outline of Vocational Education*, Huang pointed out: “The division of labor inherent in modern society necessitates a focus on enhancing work efficiency and identifying and nurturing individuals’ innate nature and talents, aligning them with suitable careers. This is the fundamental premise of vocational education". The "innate nature and talents" mentioned here imply the concept of individuality. Huang also emphasized the need to "use educational methods to enable everyone to obtain life's necessities and enjoyment according to their individuality, while fulfilling their obligations to the community". This illustrates the close relationship between vocational education and personal development.

wèi gè rén móu shēng zhī zhǔn bèi zhè yī zhí yè jiào yù de mù dì　　zài dāng nián zāo dào yǒu
为个人谋生之准备这一职业教育的目的，在当年遭到有

xiē rén de bǐ shì　　tā men dǐ huǐ zhí yè jiào yù wéi　　dàn fàn jiào yù　　wèi cǐ　huáng
些人的鄙视。他们诋毁职业教育为"啖饭教育"，为此，黄

xiān shēng zhǐ chū　　gǒu bìng gè rén shēng huó zhī lì ér bù jù　　ér shàng yǔ yán jīng shén shì yè
先生指出："苟并个人生活之力而不具，而尚与言精神事业

hū　　ér shàng yǔ yán shè huì shì yè hū　　zhí yè jiào yù zhī xiào néng　fēi zhǐ wèi gè rén
乎，而尚与言社会事业乎？职业教育之效能，非止为个人

móu shēng huó　　ér gè rén gù míng míng jí yǐ dé shēng huó zhě　　yǐ dàn fàn jiào yù gài zhí yè
谋生活，而个人固明明藉以得生活者。以啖饭教育概职业

jiào yù　　qí shuō gù shī zhī cū fú　　gāo shì zhí yè jiào yù　　nǎi zhì báo dàn fàn wèn tí
教育，其说固失之粗浮；高视职业教育，乃至薄啖饭问题

ér bù yán　　qí shuō yì lín yú xū jiāo　　zhè jīng bì de shuō míng le zhí yè jiào yù bì xū
而不言，其说亦邻于虚骄。"这精辟地说明了职业教育必须

shǐ rén jù yǒu cóng shì yī dìng zhí yè láo dòng lái móu shēng de néng lì　　fǒu zé jiù tán bú shàng
使人具有从事一定职业劳动来谋生的能力，否则就谈不上

jīng shén shì yè hé shè huì shì yè
精神事业和社会事业。

The goal of equipping individuals for making a living was scorned by some people at that time. They disparaged vocational education as "education for food". In response, Huang stated that "if one does not possess the ability to sustain one's own life, how can one talk about spiritual pursuits or social undertakings? The effectiveness of vocational education extends far beyond simply providing a means of subsistence; it is, in fact, the very foundation upon which individuals build their lives. To equate vocational education with 'education for food' is a crude and superficial view; to overly elevate it while neglecting its essential role in securing livelihoods is equally misguiding and arrogant". This eloquently explains that vocational education must equip individuals with the ability to engage in certain types of labor to make a living, otherwise spiritual pursuits and social undertakings are out of the question.

为个人服务社会之准备和为个人谋生之准备是密切结合着的。任何一种职业劳动都有二重性，既为个人谋生，又为社会服务。所以黄先生反复说明：职业“包含对己谋生与对群服务，实是一物两面。故职业教育，于整个的人生修养上乃至于国家观念、民族意义之培养上，不但毫无抵触，而且有很大的贡献”。

Fostering a sense of social responsibility is closely connected to equipping individuals with the skills to earn a living. Any type of vocational labor has a dual nature: it not only provides a livelihood for individuals but also serves society. Therefore, Huang repeatedly explained that vocation "includes both earning a living for oneself and serving the community, which are two sides of the same coin. Hence, vocational education, in the overall cultivation of life and even in the cultivation of national concepts and national significance, not only has no conflict but also makes a significant contribution".

huáng yán péi xiān sheng zài dāng nián zhǔ zhāng　　zēng jiā shēng chǎn cóng jiào yù xià shǒu　　　　bǎ
黄炎培先生在当年主张"增加生产从教育下手"，把
wèi shì jiè jí guó jiā zēng jiā shēng chǎn　　què dìng wéi zhí yè jiào yù de yí gè zhòng yào mù
"为世界及国家增加生产"确定为职业教育的一个重要目
dì　　zhè yàng zhòng shì fā zhǎn shēng chǎn lì　　zhè yàng míng què de tí chū jiào yù wèi jīng jì fú
的。这样重视发展生产力，这样明确地提出教育为经济服
wù　　zài wǒ guó shì　　dì yī shēng　　tā zài dāng nián yán jiū le dì yī cì shì jiè dà zhàn
务，在我国是"第一声"。他在当年研究了第一次世界大战
hòu gè guó jiào yù fā zhǎn de qū shì hòu　　dòng chá dào　　suǒ wèi zhàn hòu jiào yù zhě　　shēng
后各国教育发展的趋势后，洞察到"所谓战后教育者，生
chǎn jiào yù ér yǐ　　tóng shí zhǐ chū zēng jìn shēng chǎn lì jiù shì yào bǎ　　dì lì　　wù
产教育而已"，同时指出增进生产力就是要把"地力、物
lì　　rén lì níng jù qǐ lái　　ér rén lì shì yí qiè lì de zhōng xīn　　lián jì dào wǒ
力、人力凝聚起来，而人力是一切力的中心"。联系到我
guó　　tā shuō　　tǔ dì rú cǐ zhī dà　　rén kǒu rú cǐ zhī duō　　gǒu bù jí jí yān zì
国，他说："土地如此之大，人口如此之多，苟不亟亟焉自
móu suǒ yǐ zēng jìn qí shēng chǎn lì　　tā rén jiāng yǒu dài wéi móu zhě　　shì gù wú guó zhī zhàn
谋所以增进其生产力，他人将有代为谋者。是故吾国之战
hòu jiào yù　　gèng shě zhí yè jiào yù wú suǒ wéi jì　　duō nián lái de lì shǐ shì shí zhèng míng
后教育，更舍职业教育无所为计。"多年来的历史事实证明
huáng xiān sheng dāng nián zhè xiē lùn duàn de yì yì shì hěn shēn yuǎn de
黄先生当年这些论断的意义是很深远的。

Huang advocated for "increasing production through education" and established "increasing production for the world and the nation" as an important goal of vocational education. Such emphasis on developing productivity and explicitly proposing that education should serve the economy was groundbreaking in China. After studying the trends in educational development in various countries after World War I, he observed that "the so-called post-war education is essentially production education". He also pointed out that increasing productivity means "bringing together land, resources, and human power, with human power being the center of all forces". Relating this to China, he said that "with such a vast land and such a large population, if we do not urgently seek ways to increase our productivity, others will do it for us. Therefore, for China's post-war education, there is no other option but vocational education". The historical facts of many years have proven the profound significance of these statements made by Huang.

黄先生提出的职业教育目的，在旧中国固然很难完全实现。但是，在当时，这样系统地从四个方面阐明职业教育的目的，打破了就教育论教育的传统观念，确实是很大的进步。这对我们今天从人的个性发展和社会生产力的增长等多方面来提高对职业教育功能的认识，充分发挥职业教育为社会主义现代化建设服务的作用是很有助益的。

The goals of vocational education proposed by Huang were certainly difficult to fully achieve in old China. However, at that time, systematically explaining the goals of vocational education from four aspects, breaking the traditional concept of education for education's sake, was indeed a significant advancement. This is very helpful for us today to enhance our understanding of the functions of vocational education from multiple perspectives, such as personal development and the growth of social productivity, and to fully utilize vocational education to serve socialist modernization.

3) guān yú zhí yè jiào yù de shí shī fāng zhēn
3) 关于职业教育的实施方针

Implementation Strategies for Vocational Education

zěn yàng shí shī zhí yè jiào yù　　bàn hǎo zhí yè xué xiào de qí tā jiào yù shì yè　huáng
怎样实施职业教育，办好职业学校的其他教育事业。黄
xiān sheng tí chū le míng què de fāng zhēn　zhǔ yào shì shè huì huà　kē xué huà　píng mín huà
先生提出了明确的方针，主要是社会化、科学化、平民化。

Regarding how to implement vocational education and manage vocational schools and other educational undertakings, Huang proposed clear guidelines, primarily emphasizing the integration of vocational education with societal needs, a scientific approach to curriculum development, and accessibility for the general public.

huáng xiān sheng jīng guò diào yán kǎo chá hé zì jǐ bàn xué de shí jiàn jīng yàn　dé chū yī gè
黄先生经过调研考察和自己办学的实践经验，得出一个
jié lùn　lí shè huì wú jiào yù　yù dìng suǒ shī wéi hé zhǒng jiào yù　bì chá suǒ chǔ wéi
结论："离社会无教育。欲定所施为何种教育，必察所处为
hé zhǒng zhī shè huì　1930 nián　tā zài　zhí yè jiào yù jī guān wéi yī de shēng mìng shì
何种之社会。"1930年，他在《职业教育机关惟一的生命是
zěn me　yī wén zhōng zhǐ chū　zhí yè xué xiào yǒu zuì jǐn yào de yī diǎn　pì rú rén shēn
怎么》一文中指出："职业学校有最紧要的一点，譬如人身
zhòng de líng hún　dé zhī zé shēng　fú dé zé sǐ　shì shén me dōng xi ní　cóng qí běn
中的灵魂，得之则生，弗得则死。是什么东西呢？从其本

质说来，就是社会性；从其作用说来，就是社会化。”他认为：“职业学校的基础是完全筑在社会的需要上。”办什么样的学校，设置什么样的学科，怎样确定修业年限，设置怎样的课程等问题，都要调查了解当地社会生产和人民生活的需要，然后作决定。为了贯彻职业教育社会化的方针，他力求使职业教育的一切设施在都适合于社会需要的同时，还努力促成社会各方的协作，靠社会各方的力量来办各种形式的职业教育。

Through research, investigation, and his own experience in running schools, Huang concluded that "there is no education without society. To determine what kind of education to implement, one must examine what kind of society one is in". In 1930, in his article *The Lifeblood of Vocational Education Institutions*, he pointed out that "there is a crucial element in vocational schools, akin to the soul in the human body, that determines its success or failure. What is it? In essence, it is social relevance; in function, it is the integration of education with society". He believed that "the foundation of vocational schools is entirely built on the needs of society". Questions such as what kind of schools to establish, what subjects to set up, how to determine the length of study, and what curriculum to design should all be decided after investigating and understanding the needs of local social production and people's lives. To implement the guideline of socializing vocational education, he strived to make all aspects of vocational education meet the needs of society while also promoting collaboration among various sectors of society, relying on the strength of all parties to run various forms of vocational education.

黄先生在强调职业教育社会化的同时，十分重视职业教育的科学化和平民化。他认为“新教育所表现的特色只有两点，一是科学化，一是平民化。”他还指出：“职业教育，却与两者成连锁的形势。就是一方要用科学来解决职业教育问题，一方要用职业教育来解决平民问题。”他认为，有关职业和职业教育的问题都要用科学来解决。他在这里讲的科学是比较广泛的，包括工业和农业等物质生产活动中所包含的各种科学技术，工厂、商店、学校和各种机关的科学管理，还有如心理学、教育学等。为了使职业教育科学化，他十分重视科学实验。中华职业教育社推行一项职教事业时，必先进行实验研究，取得成效和经验，而后谋求推广。如创办中华职业学校是为了以例示人。该学校成立后举行过十多次专家会议，研讨有关职业教育的

zhòng yào wèn tí jìn ér cù shǐ zhí yè jiào yù kē xué huà
重要问题，进而促使职业教育科学化。

While emphasizing the integration of vocational education with societal needs, Huang also attached great importance to the scientific approach and accessibility for the general public. He believed that "the new education exhibits only two characteristics: scientific approach and public accessibility". He further pointed out that "vocational education is intertwined with both. On the one hand, we need to use science to solve the problems of vocational education, and on the other hand, we need to use vocational education to solve the problems of ordinary people". He believed that all issues related to vocations and vocational education should be addressed scientifically. The science he referred to here was broad, encompassing various scientific and technological aspects of material production activities such as industry and agriculture, scientific management of factories, stores, schools, and various institutions, as well as psychology and pedagogy. To make vocational education scientific, he emphasized scientific experimentation. Before promoting a vocational education project, the CVEA would first conduct experimental research, achieve results and gain experience, and then seek to expand it. For example, the establishment of the Zhonghua Vocational School was intended to serve as a model. After its establishment, the school held more than ten expert meetings to discuss important issues related to vocational education, thereby promoting its scientific approaches.

huáng xiān sheng yī guàn zhǔ zhāng zhí yè jiào yù miàn xiàng guǎng dà píng mín tā shuō rú guǒ
黄先生一贯主张职业教育面向广大平民。他说："如果

bàn zhí yè jiào yù ér bù zhī zhuó yǎn zài dà duō shù píng mín shēn shang tā de jiào yù wú
办职业教育而不知着眼在大多数平民身上，他的教育，无
yǒu shì chù jí bàn zhí yè jiào yù yì wú yǒu shì chù wèi le shǐ zhí yè jiào yù wèi
有是处，即办职业教育，亦无有是处。”为了使职业教育为
píng mín fú wù tā chuàng bàn zhōng huá zhí yè xué xiào shí bǎ dì zhǐ xuǎn zài shàng hǎi xī nán
平民服务，他创办中华职业学校时，把地址选在上海西南
de píng mín qū duì pín kǔ rén jiā de zǐ nǚ jiǎn miǎn xué fèi zhōng huá zhí jiào shè zài chéng
的平民区，对贫苦人家的子女减免学费。中华职教社在城
shì bàn de zhí yè bǔ xí xué xiào cǎi qǔ chén bān yè bān hé shàng mén jiāo děng duō zhǒng xíng
市办的职业补习学校采取晨班、夜班和上门教等多种形
shì biàn lì yī bān zhí gōng xué xí dāng nián huáng xiān sheng děng zhī suǒ yǐ néng gòu zài hěn kùn
式，便利一般职工学习。当年黄先生等之所以能够在很困
nan de tiáo jiàn xià jiān chí bàn xué chú le dé dào mín zú gōng shāng yè zhě de zī zhù wài
难的条件下坚持办学，除了得到民族工商业者的资助外，
hái dé yì yú píng mín qún zhòng de yōng hù
还得益于平民群众的拥护。

Huang consistently advocated making vocational education accessible to the general public. He said that "if vocational education is not focused on the majority of ordinary people, it will be useless, which makes running vocational schools pointless". To ensure vocational education serves the common people, he chose to establish the Zhonghua Vocational School in the working-class district of southwest Shanghai and offered reduced or waived tuition fees for children from poor families. The CVEA also organized various forms of vocational supplementary schools in cities, such as morning and evening classes and door-to-door teaching, to facilitate learning for ordinary workers. The reason why Huang and others were able to persist in running schools under difficult conditions was not only due to the financial support from national industrialists and businessmen but also the support from the general public.

huáng xiān sheng duì yú zhí yè jiào yù de jī běn hán yì mù dì hé shí shī fāng zhēn de lùn
黄先生对于职业教育的基本含义、目的和实施方针的论
shù shì tā de zhí yè jiào yù sī xiǎng hé shí jiàn jīng yàn de jī běn nèi róng cǐ wài
述，是他的职业教育思想和实践经验的基本内容。此外，
rú tā yī guàn tí chàng de zhí yè jiào yù yǔ shí yè jié hé shǒu nǎo bìng yòng gōng
如他一贯提倡的"职业教育与实业结合""手脑并用""工
dú jié hé hé xué xí yī guàn hù jìn fǎ děng yě yǒu zhù yú jīn tiān wǒ men gǎi
读结合"和"学习一贯互进法"等，也有助于今天我们改
jìn zhí yè jiào yù de jiào xué fāng fǎ bìng yōu huà jiào xué liú chéng
进职业教育的教学方法并优化教学流程。

Huang's discussions on the basic meaning, goals, and implementation strategies of vocational education constitute the core of his vocational education philosophy and practical experience. In addition, his consistent advocacy of "combining vocational education with industry", "combining intellectual and manual labor", "combining work and study", and the "continuous and interactive learning method" is also helpful for us today to improve vocational education teaching methods and optimize the teaching process.

3. gāo shàng lián jié, qiú zhēn wù shí, yǔ shí jù jìn, fèn dòu bù xī 高尚廉洁，求真务实，与时俱进，奋斗不息 Maintaining Integrity, Pursuing Truth, Advancing with the Times, and Striving Relentlessly

gāo shàng lián jié de rén gé qiú zhēn wù shí de sī xiǎng zuò fēng yǔ shí jù jìn fèn
高尚廉洁的人格，求真务实的思想作风，与时俱进、奋
dòu bù xī de xiàn shēn jīng shen fēng fàn cháng cún qǐ dí hòu rén
斗不息的献身精神，风范长存，启迪后人。

Huang's noble and honest character, his pragmatic and truth-seeking work ethic, and his dedication to keeping pace with the times and striving relentlessly, all serve as an enduring model and inspiration for future generations.

huáng xiān sheng zhī suǒ yǐ chéng wéi zhuó yuè de jiào yù jiā chú le nǔ lì chàng dǎo hé tuī xíng
黄先生之所以成为卓越的教育家，除了努力倡导和推行
zhí yè jiào yù de zhuó yuè gòng xiàn wài hái jī yú tā wèi guó wèi mín de rén shēng zōng zhǐ
职业教育的卓越贡献外，还基于他为国为民的人生宗旨，
gāo shàng lián jié de rén gé qiú zhēn wù shí de sī xiǎng zuò fēng yǔ shí jù jìn fèn dòu
高尚廉洁的人格，求真务实的思想作风，与时俱进、奋斗
bù xī de xiàn shēn jīng shen jí zhōng tǐ xiàn chū rén mín jiào yù jiā de chóng gāo pǐn zhì tā
不息的献身精神，集中体现出人民教育家的崇高品质。他
de zhuó yuè gòng xiàn hé tā de chóng gāo pǐn zhì shì jié hé zài yī qǐ de
的卓越贡献和他的崇高品质是结合在一起的。

Huang's success as an outstanding educator stemmed not only from his tireless advocacy and promotion of vocational education but also from his dedication to serving the country and its people. His noble and honest character, his pragmatic and truth-seeking work ethic, and his dedication to keeping pace with the times and striving relentlessly, all embodied the noble qualities of a true educator of the people. His remarkable contributions and his noble character were intertwined.

huáng xiān sheng zài bā shí nián lái zì xù zhōng shuō yī fēn jīng shen quán wèi guó
黄先生在《八十年来》自序中说："一分精神全为国，
yī cùn guāng yīn quán wèi mín kě jiàn wèi guó wèi mín shì tā de rén shēng zōng zhǐ tā hé
一寸光阴全为民。"可见，为国为民是他的人生宗旨。他和
zhōng huá zhí yè jiào yù shè de shì yè jǐn guǎn jīng lì guò bù shǎo qū zhé hé kùn nan yě
中华职业教育社的事业，尽管经历过不少曲折和困难，也
bù miǎn yǒu shī wù dàn shǐ zhōng méi yǒu lí kāi guò wèi guó wèi mín zhè ge rén shēng zōng zhǐ
不免有失误，但始终没有离开过为国为民这个人生宗旨。

黄先生为国为民的人生宗旨是和他高尚廉洁的人格融为一体的。他早年考中了举人，本有高官厚禄可图，但他在南洋公学被解散后，献身教育事业，回乡创办川沙小学堂。因学堂经费极为困难，他不取分文薪水，靠乡试中试“朱卷”收入维持着十分清苦的生活。中华职业教育社成立后，他尽心尽力于职教事业。这期间，北洋政府曾两次任命他为教育总长，他拒不受命。为了使中华职教社按照计划开展工作，他多方奔走，筹募经费。他对列强在中国占有租界深感愤恨，从不住租界，长期住在上海南市一栋小楼的厢房里。后来他用筹募来的经费为中华职教社建造了公用大楼，自己却仍住在那间厢房里。他从不添置家产，卧室就是会客室。

In the preface to his work *The Past Eighty Years*, Huang stated that “all my energy is dedicated to the country, every moment is dedicated to the people”. It is evident that serving the country and its people was his lifelong purpose. Throughout his career and the endeavors of the CVEA, despite facing numerous setbacks and difficulties, and even occasional mistakes, he never deviated from this pursuit. Huang’s dedication to the nation and its people was inseparable from his noble and honest character. In his early years, he passed the imperial examination and could have pursued a lucrative official career. However, after the disbandment of Nanyang Public School, he chose to devote himself to education, returning to his hometown to establish Chuansha Primary School. Due to the school's financial difficulties, he refused to take any salary and relied on the meager income from selling his successful imperial examination essay copies to maintain a frugal life. After the establishment of the CVEA, he dedicated himself to the cause of vocational education. During this time, the Beiyang Government twice appointed him as Minister of Education, but he declined both offers. To ensure the smooth progress of the CVEA's work, he traveled extensively to raise funds. He deeply resented the foreign powers' occupation of concessions in China and refused to live in them, residing for a long time in a small room in a building in Shanghai's Nanshi district. Later, he used the funds raised to build a public building for the CVEA but continued to live in that small room. He never accumulated personal wealth, and his bedroom served as his reception room.

kàng rì zhàn zhēng quán miàn bào fā hòu zhōng huá zhí yè jiào yù shè qiān dào chóng qìng guó nàn
抗日战争全面爆发后，中华职业教育社迁到重庆。国难

qī jiān huáng xiān sheng hé zhōng huá zhí jiào shè tóng zhì gèng wéi qín jiǎn jié yuē yī dù diàn yī
期间，黄先生和中华职教社同志更为勤俭节约，一度电一

dī shuǐ dōu bù làng fèi nǎi zhì yú duì yòng guò de xìn fēng yě yào fān guò lái zài yòng kàng
滴水都不浪费，乃至于对用过的信封也要翻过来再用。抗

zhàn shèng lì hòu tā suí zhōng huá zhí jiào shè zǒng shè qiān huí shàng hǎi zhè qī jiān guó tǒng
战胜利后，他随中华职教社总社迁回上海。这期间，国统

qū wù jià fēi zhǎng mín bù liáo shēng huáng xiān sheng bù dé bù yǐ biàn mài cáng shū mài zì
区物价飞涨，民不聊生。黄先生不得不以变卖藏书，卖字

yǐ zī shēng huó   tā mài zì yě bù wàng jiào yù   bù wàng jiù guó   xiě de shì shī piān hé

以资生活。他卖字也不忘教育、不忘救国，写的是诗篇和

gé yán   tā zài   wǔ dǒu gē   zhōng jiǎng míng   yī lián yī fú yī shàn mǐ wǔ dǒu   yì

格言。他在《五斗歌》中讲明："一联一幅一扇米五斗。益

rén shēn yǔ xīn   fēi tú hú wǒ kǒu   tā hái xiě le tí wèi   yù zì   de shī

人身与心，非徒糊我口。"他还写了题为《鬻字》的诗：

lǎo lái yù zì shì hé yīn   bù huì yán pín wèi liáo pín   shāng lián gǒu qǔ chéng cán

"老来鬻字是何因，不讳言贫为疗贫。……伤廉苟取诚惭

kuì   shí lì yòng shū yì kǔ xīn   shū fā le tā tǎn zhí lián jié de qíng huái

愧，食力佣书亦苦辛。"抒发了他坦直廉洁的情怀。

After the full — scale outbreak of the War of Resistance against Japanese Aggression, the CVEA relocated to Chongqing. During this national crisis, Huang and his colleagues at the association became even more frugal, not wasting a single kilowatt — hour of electricity or a drop of water, even reusing old envelopes. After the victory of the war, he returned to Shanghai with the association's headquarters. During this period, prices in the Kuomintang — controlled areas soared, and people's lives were miserable. Huang had to sell his collection of books and calligraphy to make ends meet. Even in such poor condition, he did not forget about education or saving the country, and his poems and mottos were themed around these causes. In his *Five Dou of Rice* he explained: A couplet, a scroll, a screen, five dou of rice I charge, To nourish body and soul, not just to fill my belly's barge.He also wrote a poem titled *Selling Calligraphy*, expressing his honesty and integrity: Why do I sell calligraphy in my old age? To mend my plight, Not ashamed to admit my need, poverty's my fight.... Though honor's wounded by this trade, and shame I feel, Yet honest labor's still a toil, though writing pays my meal.

黄先生常以“理必求真，事必求是，言必守信，行必踏实”十六字格言启示别人，同时更用以规范自己，做到言行一致，以身作则。他坚持追求真理，实事求是。他当年所以提倡职业教育，是“本于自谋，非发于外铄”。由于深信推行职业教育切合于中国社会经济和人民生计的需要，所以他要求自己和职教工作者“下决心脚踏实地，用极辟实的工夫去做”。他对国家社会全局的大事，更严格做到“实事求是”。在国共之间，他先在中间当调人。经过多次事实的启示，他终于认清了孰真孰伪，走上了正确的道路。特别是延安之行亲眼看到延安没有一寸土地荒着，没有一个人闲荡，政府对每个老百姓都负责等等情况，从而更认清真理和希望所在。一回重庆，他就不顾个人安危，写成《延安归来》一书。同时他以踏实的行动，带头推动拒绝国民党反动派检查图书杂志的斗争。《延安归来》畅销各地，用事实来彰显解放区的成就，辟除诽谤解放区的谣言。他越来越看清了国民党反动派的真面目，同时日益增强了对中国共产党的信任。

Huang often used the motto "pursue truth through reasoning, verify truth with facts, honor commitments in words, and remain steadfast in actions" to enlighten others and also to regulate himself, ensuring consistency between words and actions, and leading by example. He persisted in pursuing truth and seeking truth from facts. His advocacy for vocational education was "based on self-motivation, not external pressure". With an unwavering belief that promoting vocational education must be aligned with the needs of Chinese society, economy, and people's livelihoods, he urged himself and vocational educators to adopt a "down-to-earth and diligent" work ethic. He was even more rigorous in "seeking truth from facts" when it came to major issues concerning the overall situation of the country and society. Between the Kuomintang and the Communist Party, he initially acted as a mediator. After repeated revelations of facts, he finally discerned the truth from falsehood and embarked on the right path. In particular, his visit to Yan'an allowed him to witness firsthand that not an inch of land was left uncultivated, not a single person was idle, and the government was responsible for every ordinary citizen. This further clarified the truth and where hope lay. Upon returning to Chongqing, he disregarded his personal safety and wrote the book *Returning from Yan'an*. Meanwhile, he took practical action and led the fight against the Kuomintang reactionaries' inspection of books and magazines. *Returning from Yan'an* sold well throughout the country, using facts to highlight the achievements of the liberated areas and dispel rumors that slandered them. He increasingly saw through the true nature of the Kuomintang reactionaries while his trust in the Communist Party of China grew stronger.

新中国成立后，他欣然担任政务院副总理等职。他说明："我以往坚拒做官是不愿入污泥，今天是参加中国共产党领导下的人民政府的工作，我做的是人民的官啊！"为了做好人民的官，他严于律己，廉洁奉公。他原住在简陋的四合院内，周总理亲自安排为他修建一栋小楼，然而他却一再推让。他继续保持当年勤俭节约的习惯，仍然把用过的信封翻过来再用。他深得毛泽东同志的赞扬，称之为"炎培作风"。同时他不顾年老，认真学习马列主义毛泽东思想和党的方针政策。他精读了《资本论》第一卷，参阅了《马克思传》等，写了几万字的读《资本论》心得和《马克思颂》长诗。他一面学习，一面积极主动地工作，单单写给毛泽东同志的信就有近百件。党中央和毛主席对他主动踏实的工作，给予了相当高的评价。

After the founding of the People's Republic of China, he readily accepted positions such as Vice Premier of the Government Administration Council. "I used to firmly refuse official positions because I didn't want to be tainted by the mud. Today, I am participating in the work of the People 's Government led by the Communist Party of China. I am an official of the people!" He explained. To be a good official of the people, he was strict with himself and served the public with integrity. He originally lived in a humble courtyard house, and Premier Zhou Enlai personally arranged for a small building to be built for him, but he repeatedly declined. He continued his frugal habits from earlier years, still turning over used envelopes for reuse. He was highly praised by Chairman Mao Zedong, who called it the "Yanpei Style". Despite his advanced age, he earnestly studied Marxism – Leninism, Mao Zedong Thought, and the CPC's principles and policies. He carefully read the first volume of *Das Kapital*, consulted *Karl Marx: A Biography*, and wrote tens of thousands of words of reading notes on *Das Kapital* and a long poem titled *Ode to Marx*. While studying, he actively engaged in work, writing nearly a hundred letters to Chairman Mao alone. The Party Central Committee and Chairman Mao highly praised his proactive and practical work.

huáng xiān sheng dāng nián de jiào yù sī xiǎng lǐ lùn hé jiào yù shí jiàn jīng yàn nán miǎn yǒu
黄先生当年的教育思想理论和教育实践经验，难免有
lì shǐ de jú xiàn rán ér tā wèi guó wèi mín de rén shēng zōng zhǐ gāo shàng lián jié de rén
历史的局限，然而他为国为民的人生宗旨，高尚廉洁的人
gé pǐn zhì qiú zhēn qiú shì wù shí de sī xiǎng zuò fēng yǔ shí jù jìn fèn dòu
格品质，求真、求是、务实的思想作风，与时俱进、奋斗
bù xī de xiàn shēn jīng shén bì jiāng fēng fàn cháng cún qǐ dí hòu rén zhè xiē yōu liáng zuò
不息的献身精神，必将风范长存，启迪后人。这些优良作
fēng hé guāng huī jīng shén duì wǒ men dāng qián hé jīn hòu de shè huì zhǔ yì jīng shén wén míng jiàn shè
风和光辉精神对我们当前和今后的社会主义精神文明建设
hé lián zhèng jiàn shè jù yǒu zhòng dà de xiàn shí yì yì
和廉政建设具有重大的现实意义。

Huang's educational thought, theory, and practical experience inevitably had historical limitations. However, his lifelong purpose of serving the country and its people, his noble and honest character, his pragmatic and truth–seeking approach, and his spirit of keeping pace with the times and striving relentlessly will forever be remembered and inspire future generations. These excellent qualities and shining spirit hold great practical significance for our current and future socialist ideological and ethical progress and anti–corruption efforts.

huáng yán péi xiān sheng zhēn yán ruì yǔ

4. 黄炎培先生箴言睿语

Wise Words and Aphorisms of Huang

huáng yán péi xiān sheng de rén shēng guān

1）黄炎培先生的人生观 Huang's Outlook on Life

xū qīng qīng bái bái de zuò rén
须清清白白地做人。

xū cóng yuǎn chù kàn cóng jìn chù zuò
须从远处看，从近处做。

wǒ shì qún yǐ shēng xū jiǎn shǎo gè rén yī qiè dǎ suàn duì qún móu jǐn liàng de gòng xiàn
我恃群以生，须减少个人一切打算，对群谋尽量的贡献。

Live a life of integrity and honesty.

Envision the distant future, but act in the present.

I rely on the community for my existence, so I must minimize personal considerations and contribute as much as possible to the community.

huáng yán péi xiān sheng de zuò yòu míng
2）黄炎培先生的座右铭 Huang's Mottos

lǐ bì qiú zhēn shì bì qiú shì yán bì shǒu xìn xíng bì tā shi
理必求真，事必求是，言必守信，行必踏实。

shì xián wù huāng shì fán wù huāng yǒu yán bì xìn wú yù zé gāng
事闲勿荒，事繁勿慌，有言必信，无欲则刚。

hé ruò chūn fēng sù ruò qiū shuāng qǔ xiàng yú qián wài yuán nèi fāng
和若春风，肃若秋霜，取象于钱，外圆内方。

Pursue truth through reasoning, verify truth with facts, honor commitments in words, and remain steadfast in actions

Remain diligent in times of tranquility, composed in times of chaos, trustworthy in words, and unwavering in the face of temptation.

Be gentle as a spring breeze, resolute as autumn frost, and like water, be adaptable yet unwavering.

dì èr piān

第二篇 Part 2

huángyán péi zhí yè jiào yù lùn xuǎn cuì

黄炎培职业教育论选粹

Selected Excerpts from Huang's Works on Vocational Education

zhí yè yǔ zhí yè jiào yù

1. 职业与职业教育

Vocations and Vocational Education

rén lèi xiān yǒu zhí yè hòu yǒu zhí yè jiào yù yīn cóng shì yú shēng huó xū qiú zhī gōng
人类先有职业，后有职业教育。因从事于生活需求之供
jǐ běn yú fēn gōng de zì rán qū shì yǎng chéng zhuān mén gōng zuò ér zhí yè yǐ xīng
给，本于分工的自然趋势，养成专门工作，而职业以兴。
qí hòu yīn shēng huó jìng zhēng rì liè móu gōng zuò zhī chuán shòu yǔ jīng jìn cái yǒu suǒ wèi zhí
其后因生活竞争日烈，谋工作之传授与精进，才有所谓职
yè jiào yù
业教育。

Initially, humans developed vocations, which subsequently led to the establishment of vocational education. Due to the natural trend of division of labor in providing for life's necessities, specialized work developed, and thus vocations arose. Later, as competition for survival intensified, the transmission and advancement of work skills led to what we call vocational education.

——黄炎培 Huang Yanpei

jiě dú
【解读】［Interpretation］

zhí yè jí gè rén suǒ cóng shì de fú wù yú shè huì bìng yǐ qí bào chou zuò wéi zhǔ
职业，即个人所从事的服务于社会并以其报酬作为主
yào shēng huó lái yuán de gōng zuò zhí yè shì zhěng gè shè huì gòu jiàn de jī chǔ zhí yè jiào
要生活来源的工作。职业是整个社会构建的基础。职业教
yù jí yǐ jiào yù wéi fāng fǎ ér yǐ zhí yè wéi mù dì de yī zhǒng jiào yù
育，即以教育为方法而以职业为目的的一种教育。

zhí yè jiào yù de suǒ yǒu gōng zuò dōu bì xū wéi rào liǎng gè hé xīn yī gè shì
职业教育的所有工作都必须围绕两个核心：一个是
yè yī gè shì rén yè jiù shì zhí yè rén jiù shì shòu jiào yù
"业"，一个是"人"。"业"就是职业，"人"就是受教育
zhě xìng bàn zhí yè jiào yù jiù shì yào lì yè lì rén zhí yè jiào yù yǔ pǔ tōng jiào
者。兴办职业教育就是要"立业立人"。职业教育与普通教
yù de bù tóng zhī chù zài yú tā qiáng diào zhí yè yǔ lì rén de guān xì tā
育的不同之处在于它强调"职业"与"立人"的关系，它
mù dì míng què qiě zhēn duì xìng qiáng jiāng rén yǔ zhí yè jǐn mì lián jì qǐ lái jiāng rén de
目的明确且针对性强，将人与职业紧密联系起来，将人的
jiào yù yǔ shè huì xū qiú jǐn mì lián jì qǐ lái
教育与社会需求紧密联系起来。

A vocation is the work that an individual engages in to serve society and earn a living. Vocations are the foundation of society. Vocational education is a type of education that uses educational methods to achieve vocational goals.

All vocational education efforts must revolve around two cores：one is "vocation", and the other is "people". "Vocation" refers to the profession or occupation, and "people" refers to the learners. The purpose of vocational education is to "establish careers and cultivate individuals". The difference between vocational education and general education lies in its emphasis on the relationship between "vocation" and "cultivating individuals". It possesses definitive objectives and marked relevance, forging a tight bond between individuals and their selected careers, while ensuring that education is directly responsive to the needs of society.

2. 职业教育的定义

Definition of Vocational Education

职业教育之定义，是“用教育方法，使人人依其个性，获得生活的供给和乐趣，同时尽其对群之义务。”为学生或在职人员学习、掌握某种生产或工作所需知识、技能等而实施的教育。

The definition of vocational education is to "use educational methods to enable everyone to obtain life's necessities and enjoyment according to their individuality, while fulfilling their obligations to the community". It is the education implemented for students or employees to learn and master the knowledge, skills, etc., required for a certain type of production or work.

jiě dú
【解读】［Interpretation］

huáng yán péi xiān sheng fǎn fù qiáng diào zhí yè de yì yì rèn wéi zhí yè jù yǒu duì yǐ móu
黄炎培先生反复强调职业的意义，认为职业具有对已谋
shēng duì qún fú wù de shuāng chóng jià zhí tā yī fāng miàn rèn wéi zhí yè shì rén lèi shēng cún
生、对群服务的双重价值。他一方面认为职业是人类生存
hé shè huì fā zhǎn de tiān rán chéng zài shì rén zuì jī běn yě zuì yǒu yì yì de shēng mìng huó
和社会发展的天然承载，是人最基本也最有意义的生命活
dòng fāng shì lìng yī fāng miàn yòu rèn wéi zhí yè jiāng rén yǔ shè huì yǒu jī de lián jì qǐ
动方式；另一方面又认为职业将人与社会有机地联系起
lái jì shǐ rén néng zài zhí yè zhōng huò dé zì wǒ shí xiàn yòu néng zài zhè zhǒng shí xiàn zhī
来，既使人能在职业中获得自我实现，又能在这种实现之
zhōng wèi zhěng gè shè huì móu fú lì cóng ér cù jìn shè huì fā zhǎn hé jìn bù
中为整个社会谋福利，从而促进社会发展和进步。

Huang repeatedly emphasized the significance of vocations, believing that they have the dual value of providing a livelihood for oneself and serving the community. On the one hand, he saw vocations as the natural carrier of human survival and social development, the most fundamental and meaningful form of life activity. On the other hand, he believed that vocations organically connect individuals with society, enabling them to achieve self – realization while contributing to the wellD – being of the entire society, thereby promoting social development and progress.

zhí yè jiào yù de mù dì
3. 职业教育的目的

Goals of Vocational Education

huáng yán péi xiān sheng rèn wéi zhí yè jiào yù de mù dì yǒu sì gè jí móu gè xìng zhī fā
黄炎培先生认为职业教育的目的有四个，即谋个性之发

zhǎn　wèi gè rén móu shēng zhī zhǔn bèi　wèi gè rén fú wù shè huì zhī zhǔn bèi　wèi guó jiā
展，为个人谋生之准备，为个人服务社会之准备，为国家

jí shì jiè zēng jìn shēng chǎn lì zhī zhǔn bèi
及世界增进生产力之准备。

Huang believed that "…vocational education has four goals: promoting individual development, equipping individuals with the skills to earn a living, fostering a sense of social responsibility, and contributing to national and global productivity."

【解读】[Interpretation]

zhí yè jiào yù bù jǐn shì wèi gè rén móu shēng de　ér qiě shì wèi shè huì fú wù de
职业教育不仅是为个人谋生的，而且是为社会服务的。
tā bǎ zhí yè dào dé jiào yù de jī běn yāo qiú guī nà wéi　jìng yè lè qún　jìng
他把职业道德教育的基本要求归纳为"敬业乐群"。"敬
yè　shì zhǐ yāo qiú xué shēng ài hào bìng xǐ huan suǒ xué xí de zhuān yè hé jiāng lái suǒ yào cóng
业"是指要求学生爱好并喜欢所学习的专业和将来所要从
shì de zhí yè　bìng péi yǎng zì jǐ liáng hǎo de zhí yè xìng qù hé zé rèn xīn　lè qún
事的职业，并培养自己良好的职业兴趣和责任心。"乐群"
zhǐ xué shēng yīng gāi yǒu liáng hǎo de tuán duì hé zuò jīng shén hé yì shí　xué huì hé tā rén xiāng
指学生应该有良好的团队合作精神和意识，学会和他人相
chǔ　xié zuò　suǒ yǐ　huáng yán péi rèn wéi zhí yè jiào yù de mù dì jiù shì yào péi yǎng
处、协作。所以，黄炎培认为职业教育的目的就是要培养
jì yǒu zhuān yè zhī shi jì néng　yòu yǒu fú wù hé fèng xiàn jīng shén de ài gǎng jìng yè de zhuān
既有专业知识技能，又有服务和奉献精神的爱岗敬业的专
mén rén cái
门人才。

Vocational education is not only for personal livelihoods but also for serving society. Huang summarized the basic requirements of vocational ethics education as "respecting one's profession and enjoying the community". "Respecting one's profession" refers to encouraging students to love and enjoy the major they are studying and the profession they will pursue in the future , cultivating good professional interests and a sense of responsibility. “Enjoying the community” signifies that students ought to cultivate a robust team spirit and consciousness , mastering the art of interpersonal relations and collaboration. Therefore, Huang believed that the goal of vocational education is to cultivate professionals who not only possess specialized knowledge and skills but also have an awareness of service and dedication, loving their jobs and respecting their profession.

4. 职业教育的宗旨

Purpose of Vocational Education

使无业者有业，使有业者乐业。

Providing employment for the jobless and cultivating job satisfaction for the employed.

——黄炎培 Huang Yanpei

【解读】［Interpretation］

就职业教育的宗旨而言，“使无业者有业，使有业者乐业”，实际上就是围绕“业”与“人”的关系，强调谋好工作，过好人生。所谓“使无业者有业”，就是要让人“立业”。没有职业，就不能在社会中找到自己的位置，也就不

néng chéng wéi shēng huó xìng fú de rén gèng bié tí lì yè suǒ wèi shǐ yǒu yè zhě lè
能成为生活幸福的人，更别提"立业"；所谓"使有业者乐

yè jiù shì yào zài lì yè de jī chǔ shàng lì rén lè yè jiù shì yào yǐ zì
业"，就是要在立业的基础上"立人"。"乐业"就是要以自

jǐ de zhí yè wéi lè jiāng zì jǐ de zhí yè dàng chéng zì jǐ de shì yè tōng guò nǔ
己的职业为乐，将自己的职业当成自己的事业，通过努

lì cóng ér huò dé shè huì rèn tóng jìn ér shí xiàn zì wǒ jià zhí yě jiù néng guò shàng
力，从而获得社会认同，进而实现自我价值，也就能过上

xìng fú shēng huó
幸福生活。

In terms of the purpose of vocational education, "Providing employment for the jobless and cultivating job satisfaction for the employed." essentially revolves around the relationship between "career" and "individuals", emphasizing finding good jobs and living a good life. "Providing employment for the jobless" means enabling people to "establish a career". Without a vocation, one cannot find their place in society, nor can they become happy individuals, let alone "establish a career". "Cultivating job satisfaction for the employed" means to "cultivate individuals" based on establishing a career. "To cultivate job satisfaction" means to find joy in one's labor, treating it as a career, and through hard work, gaining social recognition and achieving self—worth, ultimately leading to a happy life.

zhí yè jiào yù de jiào xué yuán zé
5. 职业教育的教学原则
Teaching Principles of Vocational Education

zhí yè jiào yù yīng zuò xué hé yī lǐ lùn yǔ shí xí bìng xíng zhī shí yǔ jì néng
职业教育应做学合一，理论与实习并行，知识与技能

并重。如果只注重书本知识，而不去实地参加工作，是知而不能行，不知真知。职业教育目的乃在养成实际的、有效的生产能力，欲达此种境地，需手脑并用。

Vocational education should integrate learning with practice, with theory and practice going hand in hand, and knowledge and skills equally emphasized. Merely concentrating on theoretical knowledge without engaging in hands – on experience results in a hollow understanding—knowledge in name only. Vocational education aims to nurture tangible and efficient productive skills, requiring the simultaneous application of both intellectual and manual efforts.

——黄炎培 Huang Yanpei

【解读】［Interpretation］

黄炎培先生在《我之人生观与吾人从事职业教育之基本理论》一文中曾说："从人人日常工作，即以其劳心或劳力换取生活所需求之定型动作上，用启发方式，使人人增益其智能，即知而即行之；并深明其意义，使知人生长日劳心劳力，不专为个人生活计，而在恪尽其直接对群、间接对国的神圣义务。"他认为只有通过职业教育，才能真正促使每个人报效祖国：一方面每个人在为谋取自我生存的工作中客观地为族群和国家奉献，这是职业教育培养个体技能，使其为己谋生、为群服务的结果；另一方面，职业教育不仅培养个人职业技术，还重视职业素养、道德的形成；不仅要让个体客观为群服务，还要让他们知道自己从事职业的意义，主动担负责任，恪尽对群、对国的义务。“即知而即行”具有两层含义：一是将技能知识与工作实践结合起来，知行合一；二是将道德品质（对群、对国之责任义务所生发的道德情感）与道德行为联系起来，即已有良知，知道为群、为国的意义，就在日常行为中处处笃行。黄炎培先生强调职业教育与社会的联系，主张深入具体的职业环境中去实施职业道德教育。他说：“办职业教育，不但着重职业知能，而且还要养成他们适于这种生活的习惯。”

In his article My Outlook on *Life and the Basic Theory of Our Engagement in Vocational Education*, Huang stated that “...drawing from the daily endeavors where individuals employ their intellect and labor in pursuit of life’s essentials, we must adopt an inspiring methodology that fosters intellectual growth, prompting immediate knowledge application. It’ s crucial to grasp the profound implications of this approach, recognizing that the lifelong dedication of mental and physical efforts transcends personal sustenance, embodying the noble duty to serve the community and contribute to the nation's welfare". He believed that only through vocational education can every individual truly contribute to the motherland: on the one hand, everyone objectively contributes to the community and the country while working for their own survival, which is the result of vocational education cultivating individual skills to earn a living and serve the community. On the other hand, vocational education not only cultivates individual professional skills but also emphasizes the development of professional qualities and ethics; it not only enables individuals to objectively serve the community but also makes them aware of the significance of their professions, take the initiative to shoulder responsibilities, and fulfill their obligations to the community and the country. "prompting immediate knowledge application" has two levels of meanings: First, it denotes the combination of skill and knowledge with practical work, achieving a harmonious blend of theory and practice; second, it signifies the alignment of moral integrity (the ethical sentiments engendered by duties to society and nation) with ethical conduct, implying that an individual, endowed with moral awareness of the importance of community and national service, will naturally embody these values through their everyday actions. Huang emphasized the connection between vocational education and society and advocated for implementing vocational ethics education in specific vocational environments. "In conducting vocational education, we should not only focus on professional knowledge and skills but also cultivate their habits suitable for this kind of life", he said.

zuò yòu míng

6. 座右铭 Mottos

lǐ bì qiú zhēn shì bì qiú shì yán bì shǒu xìn xíng bì tā shi
理必求真，事必求是，言必守信，行必踏实。

Pursue truth through reasoning, verify truth with facts, honor commitments in words, and remain steadfast in actions

huáng yán péi xiān sheng zuò yòu míng zhī dì yī jù
——黄炎培先生座右铭之第一句

—the First Motto of Huang

jiě dú
【解读】［Interpretation］

lǐ bì qiú zhēn shì qiáng diào miàn duì xué wen shì lǐ yào bù duàn zhuī wèn qiú dé zhēn lǐ shì bì qiú shì shì qiáng diào zuò shì yào shàn xún shì lǐ àn guī lǜ bàn shì jiǎng huà yīng dāng shǒu xìn yòng xíng dòng yīng tā ta shí shi bù qīng fú
"理必求真"是强调面对学问事理，要不断追问、求得真理；"事必求是"是强调做事要善循事理，按规律办事。讲话应当守信用，行动应踏踏实实，不轻浮。

"Seek truth in reasoning" emphasizes the need to constantly question and pursue truth when faced with knowledge and principles. "Verify truth with facts" emphasizes the importance of following logic and facts and acting accordingly when doing things. One should keep promises and act steadfastly, without being frivolous.

shì xián wù huāng　　shì fán wù huāng　　yǒu yán bì xìn　　wú yù zé gāng
事闲勿荒，事繁勿慌，有言必信，无欲则刚。

Remain diligent in times of tranquility, composed in times of chaos, trustworthy in words, and unwavering in the face of temptation.

huáng yán péi xiān sheng zuò yòu míng zhī dì èr jù
——黄炎培先生座右铭之第二句

—the Second Motto of Huang

jiě dú
【解读】［Interpretation］

méi yǒu shì qing zuò de shí hou　　róng yì yǎng chéng yōng lǎn de è xí　　zài zhè ge shí
没有事情做的时候，容易养成慵懒的恶习，在这个时

hou　　yào shí kè jǐng cè zì jǐ　　bù yào huāng fèi shí jiān　　zuò yì xiē yǒu yì yì de
候，要时刻警策自己，不要荒废时间，做一些有意义的

shì　　shì qing duō qiě fán zá de shí hou　　yì chǎn shēng jiāo zào de qíng xù　　kě néng yīn wèi
事；事情多且繁杂的时候，易产生焦躁的情绪，可能因为

jí zào chōng dòng zuò chū bù lǐ xìng de shì qing　　zhè ge shí hou　　yīng lěng jìng chén zhuó　　zuò
急躁冲动做出不理性的事情，这个时候，应冷静沉着，做

shì bù yào huāng zhāng　　shuō huà suàn shù de rén　　bié rén cái huì xiāng xìn　　kè zhì zì jǐ de
事不要慌张；说话算数的人，别人才会相信；克制自己的

sī yù　　jiān chí cāo shǒu　　cái néng biàn de gāng zhèng　　lǐ zhí qì zhuàng　　shuō chū lái de huà
私欲，坚持操守，才能变得刚正，理直气壮。说出来的话

yào shǒu xìn　　zuò shì bì xū tā shi
要守信，做事必须踏实。

When there is nothing to do, it is easy to develop lazy habits. At such times, one should always remind oneself not to waste time and do something meaningful. When faced with a multitude of things complex, it is easy to become anxious and may lead to impulsive and irrational actions. In such situations, one should remain calm and composed. People tend to trust those who keep their word, and one can become upright and confident by restraining personal desires and adhering to principles.

hé ruò chūn fēng sù ruò qiū shuāng qǔ xiàng yú qián wài yuán nèi fāng
和若春风，肃若秋霜，取象于钱，外圆内方。

Be gentle as a spring breeze, resolute as autumn frost, and like water, be adaptable yet unwavering.

huáng yán péi xiān sheng zuò yòu míng zhī dì sān jù
——黄炎培先生座右铭之第三句

—the Third Motto of Huang

jiě dú
【解读】［Interpretation］

dài rén jiē wù yào hé ǎi kě qīn xiàng chūn fēng yī yàng nuǎn rén duì péng you tóng
待人接物要和蔼可亲，像春风一样暖人，对朋友、同
shì zuǒ lín yòu shè yào jìng zhòng chéng shí píng yì jìn rén hé qi gòng shì duì
事、左邻右舍，要敬重、诚实、平易近人，和气共事；对
dài huài rén xiàng qiū shuāng yī yàng líng lì zài yuán zé shì fēi shàng yīng ài zēng fēn míng zuò
待坏人像秋霜一样凌厉，在原则是非上，应爱憎分明，做
shì yào rèn zhēn jiān chí yuán zé zì jǐ yào zuò yī gè wài biǎo suí he nèi lǐ yán
事要认真，坚持原则。自己要做一个外表随和，内里严
zhèng duì rén suí he duì jǐ yán gé de rén
正，对人随和，对己严格的人。

When interacting with others, one should be amiable and approachable, like a warm spring breeze. Be respectful, honest, and approachable to friends, colleagues as well as neighbors, working together harmoniously. Treat malicious people with the sternness of autumn frost. In matters of principle, be clear about your loves and dislikes, be meticulous in your work, and unwavering in your principles. Strive to be a person who is easygoing on the outside but firm on the inside, adaptable to others but strict with oneself.

7. 谋生与做人 Financial Independence and Personal Development

谋生与做人，二者本应同时并重，不具谋生能力，人固无以做起，具有谋生能力，而不知做人之道，必将成为自私自利之徒，更违教育之本旨矣。

Achieving financial independence and personal development should be given equal importance. Without the ability to make a living, one cannot even begin to be adecent person. However, possessing the ability to make a living without knowing how to conduct oneself will inevitably lead to selfishness, which goes against the fundamental purpose of education.

——黄炎培 Huang Yanpei

【解读】［Interpretation］

职业教育是培养技能型、应用型人才的教育，而培养具备良好职业道德和职业技能的职业工作者则是职业教育的根本任务。其课程的本质是“学习的内容是工作，通过工作实现学习”。职业教育形式的特殊性，有机地将工作和学习紧密地联系在一起，使职业教育的教育属性带有显著的职业特点，客观上决定了职业教育不仅要教会学生“谋生”，更重要的是要教会学生“做人”。“做人”就是在工作中要具有良好的职业道德，培养具备独特性格且有利于社会的人。

Vocational education aims to cultivate skilled and practical talents. The fundamental mission of vocational education is to foster professionals with robust work ethics and skills. The core of its curriculum is “learning through work and working to learn”. The distinctive nature of vocational education seamlessly integrates work and learning, endowing its educational attributes with distinct vocational features. Objectively, this dictates that vocational education should not only instruct students on how to “earn a living” but, more crucially, on how to “be a decent person”. “Being a decent person” implies having excellent work ethics in the workplace and cultivating a unique character that contributes to society.

8. 手脑并用

Combining Intellectual and Manual Labor

劳工神圣，双手万能，手脑并用。

做学合一，手脑并用，虚实互证。

Labor is sacred, hands wield infinite capability, and the mind should work with hands.

Integrate learning with doing, combine intellectual and manual labor, and verify theory with practice.

huáng yán péi
——黄炎培 Huang Yanpei

jiě dú
【解读】[Interpretation]

huáng yán péi xiān sheng bǎ　　　shǒu nǎo bìng yòng　　zuò wéi zhí yè jiào yù de　jī běn jiào xué yuán
黄炎培先生把"手脑并用"作为职业教育的基本教学原

zé　　yāo qiú xué sheng yòng zhì huì hé shuāng shǒu qù chuàng zào shè huì cái fù　　fā zhǎn shēng chǎn
则，要求学生用智慧和双手去创造社会财富，发展生产

lì　qiáng diào　　zuò xué hé yī　　jí　　yí miàn zuò　　yí miàn xué　cóng zuò zhōng xué
力。强调"做学合一"，即"一面做，一面学；从做中学，

cóng xué zhōng zuò　cóng suí shí suí dì de gōng zuò zhōng xué xí xì tǒng de zhī shi
从学中做，从随时随地的工作中学习系统的知识。"

Huang regarded "combining intellectual and manual labor" as a fundamental teaching principle of vocational education, requiring students to use their wisdom and hands to create social wealth and develop productivity. He emphasized "integrating learning with doing", which means "learning while doing, learning from doing, and learning systematic knowledge from work anytime and anywhere".

jiào yǐ chéng rén
9. 教以成人 Educating for Adulthood

kuàng jiào yù zhī wéi shì　gǎn huà zuì shén　yōu rú yǐng xiǎng　yù yǎng chéng hé děng rén
况教育之为事，感化最神，有如影响。欲养成何等人

物，一视养之者为何等人物。一教员之影响足以及数百青年。

In the realm of education, influence is most profound, like a ripple effect. The kind of person one becomes depends on the kind of person who nurtures them. A teacher's influence can reach hundreds of young people.

——黄炎培 Huang Yanpei

【解读】［Interpretation］

黄炎培先生对职业学校教师的要求，特别强调“身教重于言教”。他说：“创业非难，用人为难。况教育之为事，感化最神，有如影响。欲养成何等人物，一视养之者为何等人物”，“一教员之影响足以及数百青年”。这里强调教师的重要性，同时，对教师的“道”也提出了要求。他说，职业教育工作者“安可不用最高的热忱，包涵一切；最大的度量，容纳一切；发挥大合作的精神，做训练的方针，使受吾教育的精神方面和知能方面完全适合于人群的需要呢？。”因此，他十分重视职业学校教师、校长的人格素质；他主张“选择校长，须首重其人格”。“校长教员宜多与学生接触，乃得考察其各个之性行，而施相当之训话；若呆讲修身，空谈教育，既无深厚之感情，必不能养成正当之意志，不如就学生日所接触之事物，与其自身发现之现象，而乘机实施之训练。”

Huang placed particular emphasis on "teaching by example" in his requirements for vocational school teachers. He used to say that "starting a business is not difficult, but employing people is. In the realm of education, influence is most profound, like a ripple effect. The kind of person one becomes depends on the kind of person who nurtures them", and "a teacher's influence can reach hundreds of young people". This highlights the importance of teachers and also sets requirements for their "moral character". He said that vocational educators "must use the highest enthusiasm to embrace everything, the greatest tolerance to accommodate everything, and promote the spirit of cooperation to guide training, so that the students we educate can fully meet the needs of society in terms of both their spirit and knowledge and skills". Therefore, he attached great importance to the personal qualities of vocational school teachers and principals; he advocated that "when selecting a principal, their character should be the top priority". "Principals and teachers should have more contact with students, so as to observe their individual conduct and provide appropriate guidance. If one merely lectures on moral cultivation and talks about education without deep emotions, they cannot cultivate proper willpower. It is better to use the things that students come into contact with daily and the phenomena they discover themselves as opportunities for training".

yǐ yòng wèi zhǔ
10. 以用为主

Prioritizing Practical Application

jiāo shòu xué shēng zhī shi yīng dāng yǐ yòng wéi zhǔ xùn liàn xué shēng fù yǒu chún shóu de gōng shāng jì néng jì qiǎo péi xùn xué shēng jù yǒu láo dòng fú wù kè jǐ gōng zhèng de měi dé hé chuàng xīn jīng shén
教授学生知识应当以用为主，训练学生富有纯熟的工商技能、技巧，培训学生具有劳动服务、克己公正的美德和创新精神。

When teaching students knowledge, we should prioritize practical application, train students to have proficient industrial and commercial skills and techniques, and cultivate students' virtues of labor service, self-discipline, fairness, and innovation.

huáng yán péi
——黄炎培 Huang Yanpei

jiě dú
【解读】[Interpretation]

huáng yán péi xiān sheng rèn wéi zhí yè jiào yù yào xiǎng zhēn zhèng zuò dào wèi shè huì fú wù zhēn zhèng néng shì yìng shè huì xū yào nà me tā de jiào yù jiào xué nèi róng hé fāng shì bì xū yǔ xiàn shí shēng huó tè bié shì shè huì de shēng chǎn huó dòng jǐn mì jié hé tā zài
黄炎培先生认为，职业教育要想真正做到为社会服务，真正能适应社会需要，那么它的教育教学内容和方式必须与现实生活，特别是社会的生产活动紧密结合。他在强调职业教育应注重人格培养的同时，也强调要注重技能的训练。他强调职业教育必须注重技能，注重实用，要达到“技能纯熟”。他说：“职业教育的目标，很简单，很分明，是给人家一种实际上服务的知能，得了以后，要去实地应用的。”“职业教育，不惟着重在‘知’，尤着重在‘能’”。他认为技能要达到纯熟，那就得“手脑联动，做学合一”。在教育制度上，他倡导专科一贯、工读交替、学习互进制。他认为这种制度有利于做到学用一致，有利于知识和能力的全面培养，有利于理论和实际相结合。黄炎培先生说：“学而习，习而复学，使其所学与社会需要相配合，免蹈一般学非所用的流弊。”“学于此，习于此，所认定的知能，必较普通教育方法所得切实而熟练。”

Huang believed that for vocational education to truly serve society and adapt to its needs, its educational content and methods must be closely integrated with real life, especially with social production activities. While emphasizing the importance of character development in vocational education, he also stressed the need to focus on skills training. He emphasized that vocational education must focus on skills and practicality, aiming to achieve “proficient skills”. He said that “the goal of vocational education is very simple and clear: to provide people with practical knowledge and skills that they can apply in real — life scenarios". "Vocational education prioritizes not just the acquisition of knowledge, but also the competence to apply it effectively". He believed that to achieve proficiency in skills, one must "combine hands with mind, and integrate learning with doing". In terms of educational systems, he advocated for specialized, continuous education, alternating between work and study, and interactive learning. He believed that this system is conducive to achieving consistency between learning and application, comprehensive development of knowledge and abilities, and the integration of theory and practice. Huang said that "it is imperative to learn and practice, practice and then learn again, so that what is learned matches the needs of society, avoiding the common problem of learning without application... Through this approach of learning and practicing, the acquired knowledge and skills will be more practical and applicable than those gained through traditional education methods".

11. 以人为本 People – Oriented Approach

办理职业教育者，心须注意于个性之发展，使每一个人尽量发挥天赋之长，为国家社会效用。求学必求当世必须之学，教人必教之为当世不可少之人。

zhí yè běn shēn jù yǒu shuāng chóng yì yì yī shì bāo kuò duì jǐ móu shēng hé duì qún fú
职业本身具有双重意义：一是包括对己谋生和对群服
wù shí shì yī wù liǎng miàn èr shì wài shì yú shè huì fēn gōng zhì dù zhī xū yào nèi
务，实是一物两面；二是外适于社会分工制度之需要，内
yìng tiān shēng rén lèi bù qí cái xìng zhī tè zhēng
应天生人类不齐才性之特征。

jiào yù yǐ rén wéi běn bù shì bǎ kè běn huò xué xiào zuò běn wèi yì bù shì
教育以“人”为本。不是把课本或学校做本位，亦不是
bǎ dì fāng huò guó jiā zuò běn wèi yǐ rén wéi běn biàn shì wèi rén ér jiào
把地方或国家做本位……以人为本，便是为“人”而教
yù zài hái zi shēn shang yòng gōng fu jiào yù tā chéng wéi yī gè shè huì shang yōu liáng jiàn quán
育，在孩子身上用功夫，教育他成为一个社会上优良健全
de fèn zǐ
的分子。

Those who engage in vocational education should pay attention to individual development, enabling everyone to maximize their innate talents and contribute to society and the country. Seek the knowledge that is essential for the present world, and teach people to become indispensable individuals for the present world.

Vocation itself has a dual meaning: first, it includes earning a living for oneself and serving the community, which are two sides of the same coin; second, it externally adapts to the needs of the social division of labor system and internally responds to the inherent differences in human talents and aptitudes.

Education must be centered on“people”. It is not based on textbooks or schools, nor is it based on regions or countries... Focusing on people means educating for the sake of “people”, putting effort into children, and educating them to become excellent and well–rounded members of society.

——黄炎培 Huang Yanpei

【解读】［Interpretation］

“以人为本”也是黄炎培先生职业教育思想的核心理念，他说：“教育以‘人’为本，不是把课本或学校做本位，亦不是把地方或国家做本位……以人为本，便是为‘人’而教育，在孩子身上用功夫，教育他成为一个社会上优良健全的分子。”黄炎培先生把“谋个性之发展”作为职业教育的首要目的。他指出：“教育专重个人而忽略社会，与仅顾社会而忘却个人，是一样错误。近代心理学对于教育一个最大的贡献，是个性的发现，使教育注意于个性的适应。一个社会人人有职业，有与其个性相适应之职业，则人人得事，事事得人，社会无有不发达者。”所以，“办理职业教育者，必须注意于个性之发展”。“使每一个人尽量发挥天赋之长，为国家社会效用。”在黄炎培先生看来，“人们大都有天赋的个性与特长，而兴趣做他的先导，一经启发着，很可能尽量地发挥出来”，“求工作效能的增进，与工作者天性、天才的认识与浚发，进而与其工作适合”。这里强调职业教育要尊重人的个性，这一观念在当时是十分先进的，已经探究到了现代教育的最高境界，已经认识到尊重学生个性发展，努力创造有利环境，促进个性发展与社会进步，才能够真正达到“有业者乐业”的境界。

“Focusing on people” is also a core concept in Huang’s vocational education philosophy. He said that “education is centered on ‘people’. It is not based on textbooks or schools, nor is it based on regions or countries... Focusing on people means educating for the sake of ‘people’, putting effort into children, and educating them to become excellent and well – rounded members of society”. Huang considered “promoting individual development” as the primary goal of vocational education. He pointed out that “education that solely focuses on individuals and neglects society, or only cares about society and forgets about individuals, is equally wrong. The greatest contribution of modern psychology to education is the discovery of individuality, making education focus on adapting to individual differences. In a society where everyone has a vocation, and a vocation that suits their individuality, then everyone has a job, every job has the right person, and society cannot but develop”. Therefore, “those who engage in vocational education must pay attention to individual development” and “enable everyone to maximize their innate talents and contribute to society and the country”. In Huang’s view, “most people have innate individuality and strengths, with interest as their guide. Once inspired, they are likely to fully develop their potential", and "the pursuit of work efficiency improvement is closely related to the recognition and development of workers' innate nature and talents, and aligning them with their work is an ideal way to vocational education". This emphasizes that vocational education should respect individual differences, a concept that was very advanced at the time and had already explored the highest realm of modern education. It recognized that only by respecting students' individual development and creating a favorable environment to promote individual development and social progress can we truly achieve the state of "those with jobs enjoying their jobs".

12. 人格与人文情怀
rén gé yǔ rén wén qíng huái

Personality and Humanistic Spirit

gāo shàng chún jié zhī rén gé，bó ài hù zhù zhī jīng shén，xiá yì yǒng gǎn zhī qì gài，
高尚纯洁之人格，博爱互助之精神，侠义勇敢之气概，
kè kǔ nài láo zhī xí guàn
刻苦耐劳之习惯。

It's vital to develop noble and pure character, a spirit of universal love and mutual aid, a chivalrous and courageous demeanor, and the habit of diligence and perseverance.

huáng yán péi
——黄炎培 Huang Yanpei

jiě dú
【解读】 [Interpretation]

chóng shàng péi yǎng rén gé hé zhí yè dào dé de rén wén qíng huái shì huáng yán péi zhí yè
崇尚培养人格和职业道德的人文情怀，是黄炎培职业

jiào yù sī xiǎng de hé xīn lǐ niàn zhī yī huáng yán péi xiān sheng qiáng diào rén gé bì xū wán
教育思想的核心理念之一。黄炎培先生强调"人格必须完

zhěng tā rèn wéi yī gè rén zài rèn hé huán jìng hé tiáo jiàn xià dōu yào kàn zhòng zì jǐ de
整"，他认为一个人在任何环境和条件下，都要看重自己的

rén gé jià zhí tā rèn wéi zhǐ yǒu jù bèi mèng zǐ suǒ shuō de fù guì bù néng yín pín
人格价值。他认为只有具备孟子所说的"富贵不能淫，贫

jiàn bù néng yí wēi wǔ bù néng qū zhè sān gè qián tí tiáo jiàn de rén cái shì yī gè
贱不能移，威武不能屈"这三个前提条件的人，才是一个

jù yǒu wán zhěng rén gé de rén wèi cǐ tā yāo qiú qīng nián jù bèi gāo shàng chún jié zhī
具有完整人格的人。为此，他要求青年具备"高尚纯洁之

rén gé bó ài hù zhù zhī jīng shén xiá yì yǒng gǎn zhī qì gài kè kǔ nài láo zhī
人格""博爱互助之精神""侠义勇敢之气概""刻苦耐劳之

xí guàn zhè sì zhǒng rén gé xiū yǎng
习惯"这四种人格修养。

Advocating for the cultivation of personality and professional ethics with a humanistic spirit is one of the core concepts in Huang's vocational education philosophy. Huang emphasized the importance of "integrity of character", believing that one should value one's personal integrity under any circumstances. He believed that only those who possess the three prerequisites mentioned by Mencius— "not to be corrupted by wealth and honor, not to be swayed by poverty and lowliness, and not to be bent by force and power" —are individuals with complete character. To this end, he required young people to cultivate these four aspects of personal development：To develop noble and pure character, a spirit of universal love and mutual aid, a chivalrous and courageous demeanor, and the habit of diligence and perseverance.

rén gé yī jīng huǐ sǔn qí rén jiàn qì yú qún zhòng nǎ yǒu gōng míng shì yè kě yán
人格一经毁损，其人见弃于群众，哪有功名事业可言？

zì jǐ zūn zhòng rén gé tóng shí hái xū zūn zhòng tā rén rén gé hù xiāng zūn zhòng shí
自己尊重人格，同时还须尊重他人人格；互相尊重，实

wéi rén yǔ rén jiān zuì lǐ xiǎng de jìng dì
为人与人间最理想的境地。

Once a person's character is damaged, they will be abandoned by the society. How can they get fame or a career?

Respect your own character, and at the same time, respect the character of others. Mutual respect is truly the most ideal state between people.

huáng yán péi
——黄炎培 Huang Yanpei

jiě dú
【解读】［Interpretation］

huáng yán péi xiān sheng rèn wéi rén gé yī jīng huǐ sǔn qí rén jiàn qì yú qún
黄炎培先生认为："人格一经毁损，其人见弃于群

zhòng nǎ yǒu gōng míng shì yè kě yán tā gào jiè tóng xué men zì jǐ zūn zhòng rén
众，哪有功名事业可言？"他告诫同学们"自己尊重人

gé tóng shí hái xū zūn zhòng tā rén rén gé hù xiāng zūn zhòng shí wèi rén yǔ rén jiān
格，同时还须尊重他人人格；互相尊重，实为人与人间

zuì lǐ xiǎng de jìng dì tā zhǔ zhāng zhí yè jiào yù zhě tóng shí bì xū zhù chóng zhí
最理想的境地"。他"主张职业教育者，同时必须注重职

yè dào dé tā rèn wéi zhí yè jiào yù de mù dì yīng yóu gè rén móu shēng jìn ér
业道德"。他认为职业教育的目的应由"个人谋生"进而

fú wù shè huì bìng jìn qí duì rén qún de yì wù tā yāo qiú zhí yè jiào yù
"服务社会"并"尽其对人群的义务"。他要求职业教育

yīng zhù yì péi yǎng dé xìng yǎng chéng jiàn kāng rén gé jiāng lái chéng wéi shàn liáng zhī gōng mín
应"注意培养德性，养成健康人格，将来成为善良之公民"。

Huang believed that "once a person's character is damaged, they will be abandoned by society. How can they get fame or a career?" Huang warned the students that "respect your own character, and at the same time, respect the character of others. Mutual respect is truly the most ideal state between people". He advocated that vocational educators must also pay attention to professional ethics. Huang believed that the purpose of vocational education should evolve from "making a living for oneself" to "serving society" and "fulfilling one's obligations to the community". He required that vocational education should focus on cultivating virtues and developing healthy personalities, so as to become good citizens in the future.

dì sān piān

第三篇 Part 3

huáng yán péi zhí yè jiào yù shí jiàn

黄炎培职业教育实践

Huang's Practices in Vocational Education

zhōng huá zhí yè jiào yù shè

1. 中华职业教育社

China Vocational Education Association

zhōng huá zhí yè jiào yù shè shì yóu wǒ guó zhù míng ài guó mín zhǔ rén shì jiào yù jiā
中华职业教育社是由我国著名爱国民主人士、教育家
huáng yán péi xiān sheng lián hé shè huì zhī míng rén shì cài yuán péi liáng qǐ chāo zhāng jiǎn wǔ
黄炎培先生联合社会知名人士蔡元培、梁启超、张謇、伍
tíng fāng sòng hàn zhāng děng rén yú nián yuè rì zài shàng hǎi chuàng lì yǐ chàng
廷芳、宋汉章等48人于1917年5月6日在上海创立。以倡
dǎo yán jiū hé tuī xíng zhí yè jiào yù gǎi gé tuō lí shēng chǎn láo dòng tuō lí shè huì
导、研究和推行职业教育，改革脱离生产劳动、脱离社会
shēng huó de chuán tǒng jiào yù wéi zhí zhì yǐ shǐ wú yè zhě yǒu yè shǐ yǒu yè zhě lè
生活的传统教育为职志；以“使无业者有业，使有业者乐
yè wéi lǐ xiǎng tí chū zhí yè jiào yù de mù dì shì móu gè xìng zhī fā zhǎn
业”为理想，提出职业教育的目的是“谋个性之发展”，
wèi gè rén móu shēng zhī zhǔn bèi wèi gè rén fú wù shè huì zhī zhǔn bèi wèi guó jiā
“为个人谋生之准备”，“为个人服务社会之准备”，“为国家

jí shì jiè zēng jìn shēng chǎn lì zhī zhǔn bèi　　zhōng huá zhí yè jiào yù shè de chuàng lì fú hé zhōng
及世界增进生产力之准备"。中华职业教育社的创立符合中

guó shè huì shí jì de zhí yè jiào yù lǐ lùn tǐ jì　　bìng yóu cǐ kāi zhǎn de zhí yè jiào yù
国社会实际的职业教育理论体系，并由此开展的职业教育

shí jiàn　　kāi chuàng le wǒ guó jìn xiàn dài zhí yè jiào yù de xiān hé
实践，开创了我国近现代职业教育的先河。

The China Vocational Education Association（CVEA）was founded in Shanghai on May 6，1917，by Huang Yanpei, a renowned patriotic democrat and educator， along with 48 other prominent figures， including Cai Yuanpei，Liang Qichao，Zhang Jian，Wu Tingfang，and Song Hanzhang. The association was dedicated to advocating，researching， and promoting vocational education， while reforming the traditional education system， which was detached from productive labor and real－life experiences. Its vision was "To provide the unemployed with employment，and to make the employed happy in their work"， and it proposed that the goals of vocational education were to "promote individual development， equip individuals with the skills to earn a living， foster a sense of social responsibility， and contribute to national and global productivity". The establishment of the CVEA aligned with a vocational education theory system that met China's social realities，pioneering the practice of vocational education in modern China.

zhōng huá zhí yè jiào yù shè chéng lì dà huì zài shàng hǎi xī mén wài lín yīn lù jiāng sū shěng
中华职业教育社成立大会在上海西门外林荫路江苏省

jiào yù huì jǔ xíng　　tú　　wéi　　nián jiàn zài shàng hǎi huá lóng lù kǒu　　xiàn wéi shàng
教育会举行。图3-1为1930年建在上海华龙路口（现为上

hǎi shì yàn dàng lù　　hào　　de shè suǒ
海市雁荡路80号）的社所。

The inaugural meeting of the CVEA was held at the Jiangsu Provincial Education Association onLinyin Road，outside the west gate of Shanghai. Fig. 3 − 1 shows the association's office which was built in 1930 at the intersection of Hualong Road （now No. 80 Yandang Road） in Shanghai.

tú　　　　　　zhōng huá zhí yè jiào yù shè　　　　nián shè suǒ
图3-1　中华职业教育社1930年社所

Fig. 3 − 1　The CVEA office in 1930

nián　　yuè　　zhōng huá zhí yè jiào yù shè chuàng bàn le　　　jiào yù yǔ zhí yè
1917年10月，中华职业教育社创办了《教育与职业》

zá zhì　　zhè shì zhōng guó jìn dài wéi yī de zhí yè jiào yù zhuān mén kān wù　　dào　　　nián
杂志。这是中国近代唯一的职业教育专门刊物，到1949年停刊，共出版208期。1985年，该刊复刊。图3–2为《教育与职业》创刊号封面。

In October 1917, the CVEA launched the *Education and Vocation* magazine, the only periodical in modern China dedicated to vocational education. By the time it ceased publication in 1949, a total of 208 issues had been released. The magazine was revived in 1985. Fig. 3 — 2 shows the cover of the inaugural issue of *Education and Vocation*.

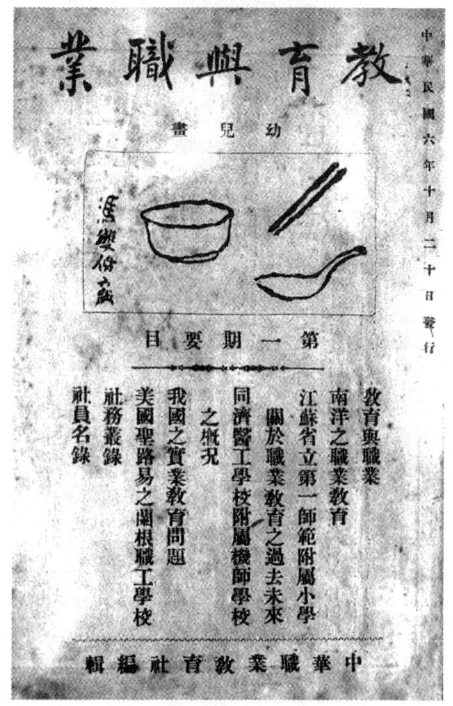

教育與職業

中華民國六年十月二十日發行

幼兒畫

第一期要目

教育與職業

南洋之職業教育

江蘇省立第一師範附屬小學關於職業教育之過去未來

同濟醫工學校附屬機師學校之概況

我國之實業教育問題

美國聖路易之藹根職工學校

社務叢錄

社員名錄

中華職業教育社編輯

图3–2　《教育与职业》创刊号封面

Fig. 3 – 2　Cover of the inaugural issue of *Education and Vocation*

1925年10月，中华职业教育社创办《生活》周刊，刊物以青年读者为对象，以职业修养和职业指导为主要内容。图3-3为《生活》周刊第一期封面。

In October 1925, the CVEA launched the *Life* weekly magazine, targeting young readers and focusing on vocational development and career guidance. Fig. 3－3 shows the cover of the first issue of *Life* weekly magazine.

民國十四年創刊

生活

生活週刊社

第一卷第一期

創刊詞

人生的矛盾

本期目次

图3-3 《生活》周刊第一期封面

Fig. 3－3 Cover of the first issue of *Life* weekly magazine

图 3–4 为位于上海华龙路（现为上海市雁荡路）的《生活》周刊社址。

Fig. 3 – 4 shows the address of the *Life* weekly magazine, located on Hualong Road (now Yandang Road) in Shanghai.

图3–4　《生活》周刊社址

Fig. 3 – 4　Address of *Life* weekly magazine

tú zhōng huá zhí yè jiào yù shè chū bǎn de bù fen zhí yè jiào yù shū jí
图3–5 中华职业教育社出版的部分职业教育书籍

Fig. 3 – 5 Some vocational education books published by the CVEA

tú shàng hǎi zhí yè zhǐ dǎo suǒ duì qiú zhí rén yuán jìn xíng xīn lǐ cè shì
图3–6　上海职业指导所对求职人员进行心理测试

Fig. 3 – 6　Shanghai Vocational Guidance Center conducting psychological tests for job seekers

tú fú wù chù gōng zuò rén yuán wèi shāng cán zhě jiè shào zhí yè
图3–7 服务处工作人员为伤残者介绍职业

Fig. 3 – 7 Service center staff introducing vocations to people with disabilities

zhōng huá zhí yè jiào yù shè zài gǎi jìn qū shè lì xīn nóng jù tuī xíng suǒ tuī guǎng xīn nóng jù qū yù dá shěng tú wéi gǎi jìn qū cūn mín shì yòng xīn nóng jù dǎ dào

中华职业教育社在改进区设立新农具推行所，推广新农具区域达15省。图3–8为改进区村民试用新农具打稻。

The CVEA established new agricultural tool promotion centers in pilot areas, and promoted new agricultural tools in 15 provinces. Fig. 3—8 shows villagers in a pilot area trying out new agricultural tools for rice threshing.

tú gǎi jìn qū cūn mín shì yòng xīn nóng jù dǎ dào
图3-8 改进区村民试用新农具打稻

Fig. 3 – 8 Villagers in a pilot area using new agricultural tools for rice threshing

2. 中华职业学校 Zhonghua Vocational School

zhōng huá zhí yè xué xiào

zhōng huá zhí yè jiào yù shè zài　　　　　nián chéng lì hòu　　jiàn yú tí chàng zhí yè jiào yù
中华职业教育社在1917年成立后，鉴于提倡职业教育

bì xū yǒu yī gè tàn suǒ lǐ lùn hé shí jiàn de shí yàn jī dì　　　yú shì　　　　nián jiù zài
必须有一个探索理论和实践的实验基地，于是1918年就在

shàng hǎi chuàng bàn le zhōng huá zhí yè xué xiào　　yǐ xià jiǎn chēng zhí xiào　　zhè shì wǒ guó jìn dài
上海创办了中华职业学校（以下简称职校），这是我国近代

shǐ shàng dì yī suǒ zhōng děng gōng shāng zhuān yè xué xiào
史上第一所中等工商专业学校。

After the establishment of the CVEA in 1917, recognizing the need for an experimental base to explore the theory and practice of vocational education, the Zhonghua Vocational School (hereinafter referred to as "the Vocational School") was founded in Shanghai in 1918. It was the first secondary—level industrial and commercial vocational school in modern Chinese history.

1) 办学宗旨和教育方针
bàn xué zōng zhǐ hé jiào yù fāng zhēn

Mission and Educational Principles

zhí xiào tí chàng xué yǐ zhì yòng hé láo dòng fú wù　　zhòng shì lǐ lùn lián jì shí jì　　yǐ
职校提倡学以致用和劳动服务，重视理论联系实际，以

láo gōng shén shèng　　shuāng shǒu wàn néng　　shǒu nǎo bìng yòng　　jìng yè lè qún　　zuò wéi jiào
"劳工神圣""双手万能""手脑并用""敬业乐群"作为教

yù de zhǐ dǎo sī xiǎng　　zài jiào yù zhōng nǔ lì gōu tōng　　jiào yù　　yǔ　　zhí yè　　dá
育的指导思想，在教育中努力沟通"教育"与"职业"，达

到“使无业者有业，使有业者乐业”的理想境界。

The Vocational School advocated learning for practical use and labor service, emphasizing the integration of theory with practice. It adopted “Labor Is Sacred”, “Hands Wield Infinite Capability”, “Combining Intellectual and Manual Labor” and “Respecting Your Profession and Enjoying the Community” as its guiding principles, striving to integrate “education” with “vocation” in practice to achieve the ideal state of “Providing employment for the jobless and cultivating job satisfaction for the employed.”.

职校创办时，黄炎培先生为职校题词“劳工神圣”。他认为“作工自养，是人们最高尚、最光明的生活”。“教育与生活、生活与教育不应脱节。”黄炎培先生又针对当时学生毕业即失业，就业而不安其所业的情况，提出“使无业者有业，使有业者乐业”的就业主张。

At the time of its founding, Huang inscribed the words “Labor Is Sacred” for the Vocational School. He believed that “working to support oneself is the most noble and brightest way of life” and that “education and life, life and education, shall not be separated”. In response to the situation at the time where students became unemployed upon graduation or were dissatisfied with their jobs, Huang proposed the employment concept of “Providing employment for the jobless and cultivating job satisfaction for the employed ".

huáng yán péi xiān sheng hái dà lì zhǔ zhāng　　shuāng shǒu wàn néng　　　tā chéng rèn gè rén yǒu gè
黄炎培先生还大力主张"双手万能",他承认各人有各

bù xiāng tóng de xìng qù yǔ néng lì　　dàn tōng guò shuāng shǒu　　gè rén dōu néng zuò gōng zì yǎng
不相同的兴趣与能力,但通过双手,各人都能作工自养,

tóng shí duì shè huì yě yǒu suǒ gòng xiàn　　suǒ yǐ tā jiān xìn kào shuāng shǒu néng chuàng zào yī qiè
同时对社会也有所贡献,所以他坚信靠双手能创造一切,

gǎi biàn yī qiè　　tā hái zhǔ zhāng　　shǒu nǎo bìng yòng　　　yào shǐ dòng shǒu de dú shū dú
改变一切。他还主张"手脑并用","要使动手的读书,读

shū de dòng shǒu　bǎ dú shū hé zuò gōng liǎng xià bìng qǐ jiā lái　　huáng yán péi　jiāng wèn yú
书的动手,把读书和做工两下并起家来"。黄炎培、江问渔

xiān sheng wèi zhí xiào zhuàn xiě de xiào gē zhōng míng què zhǐ chū　　yòng wǒ shǒu yòng wǒ nǎo bù
先生为职校撰写的校歌中明确指出:"用我手,用我脑,不

dān shì yòng wǒ bǐ　yào zuò　bù dān shì yào shuō　shì wǒ zhōng huá zhí yè xué xiào de jīn
单是用我笔;要做,不单是要说,是我中华职业学校的金

kē yù lǜ　　zhè chōng fèn biǎo míng　xué xiào de bàn xué yào zhǐ zài yú lì shuāngshǒu wàn
科玉律"。这充分表明,学校的办学要旨,在于励"双手万

néng　　shǒu nǎo bìng yòng　de kě guì jīng shén
能""手脑并用"的可贵精神。

Huang also strongly advocated for the idea that "hands wield infinite capability". He acknowledged that individuals have different interests and abilities, but through their hands, everyone can work to support themselves and contribute to society. Therefore, he firmly believed that hands can create and change everything. He also advocated for "combining intellectual and manual labor", stating that "those engaged in work should also embrace learning, and those immersed in study should also undertake work; education and work should be closely integrated". In the school song written by Huang and Jiang Wenyu, it clearly states: "Use my hands, use my brain, not just my pen; to do, not just to say, is the golden rule of our Zhonghua Vocational School". This fully demonstrates that the Vocational School's mission is to encourage the valuable spirit of "hands wield infinite capability" and "combining intellectual and manual labor".

职校按照黄炎培先生这一系列观点，提出了明确的办学宗旨："同人鉴于我国今日教育之弊病在为学不足以致用，而学生之积习尤在鄙视劳动而不屑为，致毕业于学校而失业于社会者比比。根本解决，惟有提倡职业教育，以沟通教育与职业。虽然，空言寡效，欲举例以示人，不可无实施机关，故特设此职业学校。"

Based on these ideas, the Vocational School established a clear mission: "Together with our colleagues, we acknowledge the deficiencies in our country's educational system, where theoretical knowledge often falls short in real – world application. This, coupled with a prevailing student attitude that undervalues labor and scorns manual labor, has led to a high unemployment rate among graduates. The fundamental solution is to promote vocational education to bridge the gap between education and vocation. However, mere rhetoric is insufficient; to truly lead by example, we must establish a practical implementation mechanism. This is the impetus behind the creation of our vocational school".

职校提出了明确的办学宗旨，又制定了具体的教育方针，职校教育方针的主要内容是：传授学生知识以应用为主，训练学生富有纯熟的工商技能、技巧，培养学生具有劳动服务、克己公正的美德和创新精神。教育方针有五条：

The Vocational School not only had a clear mission but also formulated specific educational principles, the main contents of which were: When teaching students knowledge, we should prioritize practical application, train students to have proficient industrial and commercial skills and techniques, and cultivate students' virtues of labor service, self—discipline, fairness, and innovation. The educational principles consisted of five points:

（1）欲求相当之职业，固不可无相当之知识，但其知识苟非十分精确，亦不足供应用。本校既以预备学生将来职业为目的，则所授各种知识，自当特别注意于应用方面，且力求正确精密，俾将来能适于应用为主。

To pursue a suitable profession, one cannot do without relevant knowledge, but if that knowledge is not very precise, it is not sufficient for application. Since our school aims to prepare students for their future careers, the various types of knowledge taught should pay special attention to practical application and strive for accuracy and precision, so that they can be applied in the future.

（2）仅有精确之知识，而无纯热之技能，则仍不足以致用。我国工商业学校生徒，往往以实习工夫之缺乏，致不能见用于社会。我校既以工商业为主，故对于实习方面特别注重，使生徒半日受课，半日实习，务期各种技能，达于纯熟为主。

Having precise knowledge without proficient skills is still not enough for practical application. Students in industrial and commercial schools in our country often cannot find employment in society due to a lack of practical experience. Since our school focuses on industry and commerce, we pay special attention to practical training, allowing students to spend half a day in class and half a day in practice, ensuring that they achieve proficiency in various skills.

（3）怠惰苟安，贱视操作服务而不屑为，亦为近今学生最大之通病。本校对于学生竭力提倡劳动服务，凡仆役所为之事，皆当由学生轮值分任；祛除其自尊自大之恶习，养成其耐劳耐苦之美德，如是则毕业后，不患其见摈于社会矣。

Laziness, complacency, and disdain for manual labor and service are also common problems among current students. Our school strives to promote labor service among students, and all tasks that servants do should be shared by students in rotation. This will eliminate their undesirable habits of arrogance and self – importance and cultivate their virtues of endurance and hard work, so that they will not be rejected by society after graduation.

（4）既得应用之知识技能，耐劳耐苦之习惯，而无善良之品性，仍不足以立身社会。故本校特注重学生自治，组织自治机关，利用共同作业，养成其共同心、责任心及勤勉诚实、克己、公正诸美德，俾将来成为善良之公民。

Having acquired practical knowledge, skills, and the habit of enduring hardship, without good character, it is still not enough to establish oneself in society. Therefore, our school pays special attention to student self – governance, organizing self – governing bodies, utilizing collaborative work to cultivate their sense of community, responsibility, diligence, honesty, self – discipline, fairness, and other virtues, so that they can become good citizens in the future.

（5）社会之事业有限，而各方之求事者日增，以学校毕业生徒而欲尽纳于社会固有之事业中，以求生活，势必不能。是故学生而无创设新事业、增进生产之能力，实不足以生存于今日之世界。本校有鉴于此，对于此点，竭力注意养成之。

The number of jobs in society is limited, but the number of job seekers is increasing day by day. It is impossible for all school graduates to find employment in existing jobs to make a living. Therefore, students without the ability to create new businesses and increase productivity cannot survive in today's world. Our school is aware of this and strives to cultivate this ability.

2）重视品德教育和职业道德教育 Emphasis on Character Guidance and Vocational Ethics Education

职校创办时，职教社明确指出：我们的职业学校，不但要培养学生具有一定的知识和技能，还必须具有良好的思想和品德。所以职校一贯重视品德教育，职校校训是“敬业乐群”，要求学生热爱祖国，热爱事业，忠于职守，胜任本职工作；并具有互助合作的精神，谦虚诚恳的态度，任劳任怨的美德，勤俭朴素的作风。

When the Vocational School was founded, the CVEA clearly stated: Our vocational schoolaim to cultivate students with certain knowledge and skills and those with good thoughts and morals. Therefore, the Vocational School has always emphasized character guidance, with the school motto being “Respecting Your Profession and Enjoying the Community”. It requires students to love their country, love their careers, be loyal to their duties, and be competent in their jobs. It also emphasizes the spirit of cooperation and mutual assistance, a humble and sincere attitude, the virtue of hard work and dedication, and a frugal and simple lifestyle.

职校特别重视爱国主义教育。鸦片战争后，我国遭受帝国主义的长期侵略，特别是“九一八”、“一·二八”事变以后，职教社领导人黄炎培、江问渔、杨卫玉等，经常到职校对学生进行时事教育；请知名人士讲述日本军国主义的本质和侵略我国的暴行；请来自东北的人士，控诉日军践踏东北同胞的罪行，以提高学生的民族自强精神，激发学生抗日救国的爱国热情。1937年全面抗战开始后，不少学生参加抗日救亡运动，或直接奔赴解放区，加入八路军、新四军等革命队伍。

The School placed particular emphasis on patriotic education. After the Opium War, China suffered long – term aggression from imperialism. Especially after the “September 18th Incident” and “January 28th Incident”, CVEA leaders such as Huang Yanpei, Jiang Wenyu, and Yang Weiyu often visited the Vocational School to educate students about current events. They invited prominent figures to explain the nature of Japanese militarism and its aggression against China, and invited people from the Northeast to denounce the atrocities committed by the Japanese army against their compatriots, aiming to enhance students' national self — reliance and stimulate their patriotic enthusiasm for resisting Japanese aggression and saving the country. After the full — scale outbreak of the War of Resistance against Japanese Aggression in 1937, many students participated in the anti — Japanese and national salvation movement or directly went to the liberated areas to join revolutionary forces such as the Eighth Route Army and the New Fourth Army.

zhí jiào duì zhí yè dào dé jiào yù yī guàn fēi cháng zhòng shì bǎ tā zuò wéi pǐn dé jiào
职校对职业道德教育一贯非常重视，把它作为品德教

yù de zhòng yào nèi róng wèi cǐ zhì dìng le shí sān tiáo xiū yǎng biāo zhǔn
育的重要内容，为此制定了十三条修养标准：

dui zhí yè zhī xìng zhì yīng yǒu zhǔn què zhī guān niàn
（1）对职业之性质应有准确之观念；

dui suǒ yù rù zhī zhí yè shè huì yīng yǒu xiāng dāng de liǎo jiě
（2）对所欲入之职业社会应有相当的了解；

dui jiāng cóng shì zhī zhí yè yīng jù yǒu xiāng dāng zhī xìng qù
（3）对将从事之职业应具有相当之兴趣；

yǎng chéng fù zé zhī xí guàn
（4）养成负责之习惯；

yǎng chéng hé zuò hù zhù de jīng shén
（5）养成合作互助的精神；

yǎng chéng qín pǔ de xí guàn
（6）养成勤朴的习惯；

yǎng chéng hé lǐ de fú cóng xí guàn
（7）养成合理的服从习惯；

yǎng chéng yǒu lǐ mào de xí guàn
（8）养成有礼貌的习惯；

yǎng chéng shǒu fǎ de xí guàn
（9）养成守法的习惯；

yǎng chéng gōng ér wàng sī de dé xìng
（10）养成公而忘私的德性；

yǎng chéng chuàng zào yǔ fèn dòu de jīng shén
（11）养成创造与奋斗的精神；

yǎng chéng yìng fù yī qiè de néng lì
（12）养成应付一切的能力；

yǎng chéng xiàn dài gōng mín suǒ yīng jù de dé xìng yǔ xí guàn
（13）养成现代公民所应具的德性与习惯。

The Vocational School consistently attached great importance to vocational ethics education, considering it an essential part of character education. For this purpose, it established thirteen cultivation standards:

1) Have a clear understanding of the nature of the profession;

2) Have a good understanding of the society in which the profession is desired;

3) Have a considerable interest in the profession to be pursued;

4) Develop the habit of responsibility;

5) Develop the spirit of cooperation and mutual assistance;

6) Develop the habit of diligence and thrift;

7) Develop the habit of reasonable obedience;

8) Develop the habit of politeness;

9) Develop the habit of law—abiding;

10) Develop the virtue of selflessness;

11) Develop the spirit of creativity and perseverance;

12) Develop the ability to cope with everything;

13) Develop the virtues and habits that modern citizens should possess.

péi yǎng zhí yè dào dé de bàn fǎ yī shì zài kè táng shàng jié hé yǒu guān jiào cái jìn
培养职业道德的办法，一是在课堂上结合有关教材进

xíng èr shì lì yòng xiào nèi wài shí xí de jī huì jìn xíng nián shāng kē xué shēng dào
行，二是利用校内外实习的机会进行。1925年商科学生到

shāng wù yìn shū guǎn mén shì bù zuò shí xí diàn yuán gāi guǎn bù gào pái shàng gōng bù jīn rì
商务印书馆门市部做实习店员，该馆布告牌上公布"今日

yóu zhōng huá zhí yè xué xiào xué shēng lái guǎn shí xí běn guǎn gè bù mén jūn yóu shí xí xué shēng
由中华职业学校学生来馆实习，本馆各部门均由实习学生

wèi gù kè fú wù gù kè jìn guǎn zhǐ jiàn nán tóng xué chuān zhe huī sè xiào fú nǚ tóng
为顾客服务"。顾客进馆，只见男同学穿着灰色校服，女同

xué chuān zhe shì lín bù qí páo shēn shang dū bié zhe shuāng shǒu wàn néng de xiào huī jiē
学穿着士林布旗袍，身上都别着"双手万能"的校徽；接

dài gù kè shí tài dù hé ǎi gōng zuò nài xīn fú wù zhōu dào jié shù shí yī yī
待顾客时，态度和蔼，工作耐心，服务周到；结束时一一

diǎn jiāo qīng chu yǐn qǐ dāng shí shè huì de qiáng liè fǎn xiǎng
点交清楚，引起当时社会的强烈反响。

The methods for cultivating professional ethics included incorporating relevant teaching materials in the classroom and utilizing opportunities for on — campus and off — campus internships. In 1925, business students interned as salespeople at the Commercial Press retail store. The store posted a notice stating："Today, students from Zhonghua Vocational School are here for internships. All departments in the store will be served by intern students". When customers entered the store, they saw male students wearing gray school uniforms and female students wearing iondanthren cheongsams, all with the school badge of "Hands Wield Infinite Capability". They greeted customers with a friendly attitude, worked patiently, and provided attentive service. At the end of the day, they carefully handed over their duties, causing a strong response in society at the time.

职校的品德教育非常重视学生自治，提倡主动自治。黄炎培先生曾着重指出：“我们在训练上绝对主张提倡主动自治，很希望青年学成以后，在职业界上发展他们自己的能力。不要像从前加一鞭走一步的神气。那么职业的效能可以大大增加了。”职校的学生自治组织叫作“职业市”。他们开展多种活动：出版刊物，组织文体活动和学科竞赛，组建抗日救亡歌咏队等，并成立伙食管理委员会管理学校伙食；又将学生宿舍编成若干村，由学生自行管理。

The Vocational School's character guidance placed great emphasis on student autonomy, advocating for proactive self – governance. Huang once emphasized: “In our training, we absolutely advocate promoting proactive self – governance. We hope that after graduation, young people can develop their abilities in the professional world, not like the old way of ‘taking a step only after being whipped.’ In this way, the effectiveness of their professions can be greatly enhanced”. The student self – governing organization in the Vocational School was called the “Vocational City”. They carried out various activities: publishing journals, organizing cultural and sports activities and academic competitions, forming anti – Japanese and national salvation singing groups, establishing a food management committee to manage the school's meals, and organizing student dormitories into several “villages” for self – management.

tóng shí， zhí xiào duì xué shēng yǒu zhe yán gé de guǎn lǐ zhì dù zhì dìng liǎo yī zhěng
同时，职校对学生有着严格的管理制度，制定了一整

tào guī zhāng zhì dù biān yìn chéng xué shēng xū zhī měi gè xué sheng rén shǒu yī cè yāo
套规章制度，编印成《学生须知》，每个学生人手一册，要

qiú xué shēng zūn zhào zhí xíng lìng yī fāng miàn xué xiào duì tóng xué gè fāng miàn dōu hěn guān
求学生遵照执行。另一方面，学校对同学各方面都很关

huái ài hù jiào shī men zūn shǒu jì lǜ de tóng shí yě néng yǐ shēn zuò zé suǒ yǐ tóng
怀、爱护，教师们遵守纪律的同时也能以身作则，所以同

xué men duì xué xiào yán gé de guǎn lǐ zhì dù yě dà dōu néng zì jué zūn shǒu yǎng chéng le
学们对学校严格的管理制度，也大都能自觉遵守，养成了

zūn shī shǒu jì de xiào fēng
尊师守纪的校风。

At the same time, the Vocational School had strict management systems for students, formulating a comprehensive set of rules and regulations compiled into a Student Handbook, which was distributed to every student and they were required them to follow it. On the other hand, the school cared for and loved the students in all aspects. The teachers not only adhered to discipline but also led by example. Therefore, most students consciously followed the school's strict management system, fostering a school spirit of respecting teachers and observing discipline.

jiān kǔ chuàng yè qín jiǎn bàn xué
3) 艰苦创业，勤俭办学 Overcoming Hardships, Running the School with Diligence and Thrift

zhí xiào kāi shǐ chuàng bàn shí yī wú jīng fèi èr wú chǎng dì sān wú xiào shè
职校开始创办时，一无经费，二无场地，三无校舍，

jīng huáng yán péi xiān sheng děng rén shì duō fāng bēn zǒu hǎo bù róng yì mù dào yī bǐ kāi bàn
经黄炎培先生等人士多方奔走，好不容易募到一笔开办

费，便租定上海南市陆家浜七亩五分荒地，披荆斩棘地建造校舍。后来又购进校旁的义冢地，发动全校师生参加劳动，开辟成为运动场。1933年建造教学大楼“中华堂”，土木科学生在教师指导下参加实习，从挖土到钢筋结扎、混凝土浇捣一直到建筑完成。汗流浃背的劳动使学生从实践中学到了整套钢筋混凝土大楼的施工技术。学校添建校舍，购置设备，大都因陋就简，能节省的就节省，能自制的就自制，从不浪费一分钱。在教职工编制方面，往往一人身兼几职，没有一名冗员，没有人浮于事的现象。这种艰苦创业、勤俭办学的作风，对同学们起到了潜移默化的作用，所以职校学生，平时的生活衣着，都很朴素，为当时教育界所少见。

When the Vocational School was first established, it faced numerous challenges: lack of funding, land, and school buildings. Through the tireless efforts of Huang and others, they managed to raise some initial funds and leased a 7.5mu (approx. 1.2 acre) plot of wasteland in Lujiabang, Nanshi, Shanghai. They cleared the land and built the school buildings. Later, they purchased an adjacent cemetery and mobilized all teachers and students to participate in labor, transforming it into a sports field. In 1933, the "Zhonghua Hall" teaching building was constructed, with students from the civil engineering department participating in the construction under the guidance of teachers, from excavation to steel bar tying, concrete pouring, and finally completion. Through their sweat and labor, the students learned the entire construction process of a reinforced concrete building. The school added new buildings and purchased equipment, mostly making do with simple and readily available materials, saving wherever possible, and making their own whenever possible, never wasting a penny. In terms of staffing, one person often held multiple positions, and there were no redundant personnel or instances of people shirking their responsibilities. This spirit of hard work, entrepreneurship, and frugality had a subtle influence on the students. As a result, the students' daily attire was very simple, a rarity in the educational circles of the time.

gēn jù shè huì xū yào què dìng shè kē hé xué zhì
4) 根据社会需要确定设科和学制 Determining Courses and School System Based on Social Needs

cóng shè huì diào chá zhuó shǒu liǎo jiě rén cái xū qiú de fā zhǎn qū shì zhú bù què dìng
从社会调查着手，了解人才需求的发展趋势，逐步确定

shè kē hé zhì dìng xué zhì zhè shì zhí xiào yī tiáo hěn hǎo de jīng yàn
设科和制定学制，这是职校一条很好的经验。

Starting with social surveys to understand the development trends of talent demand and gradually determining the courses offered and formulating the school system was a valuable experience of the Vocational

School.

职校筹办时，为决定设科，对学校附近六个小学学生家长的职业进行了调查，结果是铁工最多，木工次之，所以决定设立铁工（后改称机械）、木工两科。又因当时市场充满进口的珐琅（搪瓷）、钮扣，社会上提倡国货，抵制外货，学校便设立珐琅、钮扣两科。上海一向是通商大埠，工商业很发达，各工厂、商店急需财务会计人才，所以在1920年添设商科。1930年学校鉴于“公私建筑，日益发达，土木人才需要之殷，有增无已”，又添设土木科。此外，职校还先后开设过职业教员养成科、留法勤工预备科、机械制图科、会计职业训练班、中等机械技术科、化工科和石油机械科等。在这些学科中，以机械、土木、商科三科最切合社会需要，因而开办的时间最久，成为学校的主科。

During the preparation for the Vocational School's establishment, a survey was conducted on the occupations of parents of students in six nearby primary schools to determine the courses to be offered. The results showed that ironworkers were the most common, followed by carpenters, so it was decided to establish ironworking (later renamed mechanical) and woodworking departments. As the market was flooded with imported enamelware and buttons at the time, and there was a social call to promote domestic products and boycott foreign goods, the school also established enamelware and button – making departments. Shanghai has always been a major commercial port with a developed industrial and commercial sector. Factories and shops were in urgent need of financial and accounting personnel, so a business department was added in 1920. In 1930, the school, recognizing that "public and private construction is increasingly developing, and the demand for civil engineering talents is growing", added a civil engineering department. In addition, the Vocational School also opened a vocational teacher training department, a preparatory department for work – study programs in France, a mechanical drawing department, an accounting vocational training class, a secondary mechanical technology department, a chemical engineering department, and a petroleum machinery department. Among these disciplines, mechanical, civil engineering, and business were the most in line with social needs and therefore had the longest duration, becoming the school's main departments.

职校各科的学制，根据社会需要和学生年龄进行了试验和改革。初办工科时，分甲乙两科，甲种工科招收国民学校（初级小学）毕业生和高级小学一、二年级学生（后改为招收高小毕业生），学制三年。乙种工科招收国民学校毕业生，铁工、木工科的学制为三年，珐琅、纽扣科为二年。商科创办时也定为三年一级制，招收高小毕业生，1930年以后，全校只设机械、土木和商科，都确定为六年二级制，分为初中、高中两级，各为三年，但本校初级科毕业生，可直升高二，一共读五年，称为五年一贯制，高一则专收普通初中毕业生。这种五年一贯制，在当时历史条件下，使得学生经过扎扎实实的学习，都具备了一定的基础知识和基本技能，从而可以提早就业，以有利于提高社会生产率。

The school system for each department was experimented with and reformed based on social needs and student age. Initially, the engineering department was divided into two categories: Category A enrolled graduates from primary schools and first — and second — year students from higher primary schools (later changed to only enroll higher primary school graduates), with a three — year program. Category B enrolled primary school graduates, with a three — year program for ironworking and woodworking, and a two — year program for enamelware and button — making. When the business department was first established, it was also a three — year program, enrolling higher primary school graduates. After

1930, the school only offered mechanical, civil engineering, and business departments, all with a six — year, two — level system, divided into junior high and senior high school levels, each lasting three years. However, graduates from the school's junior high could directly enter the second year of senior high, making it a five — year program, known as the "five — year consistent system". The first year of senior high was specifically for admitting graduates from general junior high schools. Under the historical conditions of the time, this five — year consistent system allowed students to acquire solid foundational knowledge and basic skills through rigorous study, enabling them to find employment earlier and contribute to improving social productivity.

5）重视基础知识教学、基本技能训练及参观和实习 Emphasis on Basic Knowledge Teaching, Basic Skills Training, Visits, and Internships

职校三十四年的教学实践，在课程设置、基本技能的训练和参观、实习等方面，积累了不少经验。现分别讲述如下。

The Vocational School's 34 years of teaching practice accumulated considerable experience in curriculum design, basic skills training, visits, and internships. These aspects are elaborated below.

（1）课程设置 Curriculum Design

职校对机械、土木、商科的课程设置，总的原则是：“所授课程以切合职业需要而适于实用为主，力避高深理论。”教学的重点是“让学生学到坚实的基础知识”，并在课堂教学中严格要求，反复巩固。

机械科1935年的课程，除文化课外，专业课有制图工作法、机构、力学、材料及材料强弱、原动机、水力学、工厂管理、电工及实验、实习。

土木科1933年的课程，除文化课外，专业课有制图、房屋结构学、力学、材料强弱、房屋设计制图、钢骨混凝土原理、钢骨混凝土计算制图、市政工程、市政工程制图、土木工程计划、建筑学、测量法及实习。

商科1933年的课程，除文化课外，专业课有珠算、商学、簿记、会计、打字、经济、商法、统计、商业实习。

从上列三科的课程来看，专业课基本上是基础课，这些基础课程，大都切合当时职业上的需要，也适合实用。

zhí xiào zài jiào xué shang yī guàn zhòng shì lǐ lùn lián xì shí jì　　tè bié zhòng shì jī běn jì
职校在教学上一贯重视理论联系实际，特别重视基本技

néng de xùn liàn hé cān guān　shí xí
能的训练和参观、实习。

The general principle for curriculum design in the mechanical, civil engineering, and business departments was: "The courses taught should be closely aligned with vocational needs and focus on practical application, avoiding advanced theories". The emphasis of teaching was on "allowing students to acquire solid foundational knowledge" and enforcing strict requirements and repeated consolidation in classroom instruction.

In addition to cultural courses, the mechanical department's curriculum in 1935 included professional courses such as drawing methodology, mechanisms, mechanics, materials and their strength, prime movers, hydraulics, factory management, electrical engineering, and experiments and internships.

In addition to cultural courses, the civil engineering department's curriculum in 1933 included professional courses such as drawing, building structural mechanics, material strength, building design drawing, principle of reinforced concrete, reinforced concrete calculation and drawing, municipal engineering, municipal engineering drawing, civil engineering planning, architecture, surveying, and internships.

In addition to cultural courses, the business department's curriculum in 1933 included professional courses such as abacus calculation, business studies, bookkeeping, accounting, typing, economics, commercial law, statistics, and business internships.

From the curriculum of the three departments listed above, it can be seen that the professional courses were mainly basic courses, which were mostly in line with the vocational needs of the time and suitable for practical application.

The Vocational School consistently emphasized the integration of theory with practice in teaching, with a particular focus on basic skills training, visits, and internships.

（2）机械科 Mechanical Department

机械科学生基本技能的训练，主要是机械制图和各工种基本操作方法。机械制图是机械科最重要的基本技能，在五年中不间断地反复练习，教师不仅要求视图准确，还要求线条清晰美观。经过严格的训练，学生的制图能力都能达到较好的水平。有的学生毕业后考入交通大学，教授看到制图画得很出色，就同意免修。各工种操作方法，在工场实习中训练，例如各种工具的使用，机械设备的操作，以及零件的加工方法等。

职校的实习工场，划分为木工场、铸工场、锻工场、钳工场、车工场五个工场，各个工场的设备比较齐全。初

jí kē xué zhì sān nián   xué shēng lún liú zài gōng chǎng de gè gè bù mén xué xí jǐ běn cāo zuò
级科学制三年，学生轮流在工场的各个部门学习基本操作

fāng fǎ   liàn xí jiǎn yì jiā gōng jì néng   dào le gāo jí kē   jiù fēn pèi zài gè gè gōng
方法，练习简易加工技能。到了高级科，就分配在各个工

chǎng cān jiā chéng pǐn zhì zào   dāng shí shí xí gōng chǎng hái wèi wài dān wèi zhì zào jī xiè   yǒu
场参加成品制造。当时实习工场还为外单位制造机械，有

xiē chǎn pǐn jiù shì yóu xué shēng cān jiā zhì zào de
些产品就是由学生参加制造的。

The training of basic skills for students in the mechanical department mainly focused on mechanical drawing and basic operation methods for various types of work. Mechanical drawing was the most important basic skill in the mechanical department, with continuous and repeated practice throughout the five years. Teachers not only required accurate views but also clear and aesthetically pleasing lines. Through rigorous training, students' drawing abilities could reach a high level. Some students, after graduation, were admitted to Jiaotong University, and professors, impressed by their excellent drawing skills, exempted them from taking drawing courses. The operation methods for various types of work were trained during workshop internships, such as the use of various tools, the operation of machinery and equipment, and the processing methods for parts.

The Vocational School's internship workshops were divided into five workshops: woodworking, casting, forging, fitting, and turning. Each workshop was equipped with relatively complete facilities. In the first three years of junior high, students rotated through various sections of the workshops to learn basic operation methods and practice simple processing skills. In senior high, they were assigned to different workshops to participate in the manufacturing of finished products. At that time, the internship workshops also manufactured machinery for external units, and some products were manufactured with the participation of students.

　tǔ　mù　kē
（3）土木科 Civil Engineering Department

tǔ mù kē de jī běn jì néng shì zhì tú hé cè liáng　　zhì tú kè chū gāo jí dōu yǒu
土木科的基本技能是制图和测量，制图课初高级都有。
jiào shī jiào xué shí　duì huà fú de bù zhì hé xiàn tiáo de lián jiē dōu yǒu yán gé de yāo qiú
教师教学时，对画幅的布置和线条的连接都有严格的要求。
　　　　tǔ mù kē de shí xí　　zhǔ yào shì cè liáng shí xí hé jiàn zhù shí xí　　cè liáng shí xí
　　土木科的实习，主要是测量实习和建筑实习，测量实习
fēn píng miàn cè liáng hé dà dì cè liáng　píng miàn cè liáng yī bān zài xiào nèi huò fù jìn dì qū
分平面测量和大地测量。平面测量一般在校内或附近地区
jìn xíng　dà dì cè liáng cháng dào háng zhōu　wú xī děng dì gēn jù bù tóng dì xíng　dì shì
进行，大地测量常到杭州、无锡等地根据不同地形、地势
jìn xíng cè liáng xùn liàn　jiàn zhù shí xí yī bān yóu jiào shī nǐ dìng gōng chéng kè tí yāo qiú xué
进行测量训练。建筑实习一般由教师拟定工程课题要求学
shēng jìn xíng shè jì liàn xí　yǒu shí xué xiào jiē shòu wài dān wèi wěi tuō de jiàn zhù shè jì hé
生进行设计练习；有时学校接受外单位委托的建筑设计和
jiān gōng yè wù　xué shēng biàn zài jiào shī zhǐ dǎo xià cān jiā shí jì gōng zuò　zēng jiā shí jiàn
监工业务，学生便在教师指导下参加实际工作，增加实践
jīng yàn
经验。

The basic skills in the civil engineering department were drawing and surveying, with drawing classes offered in both junior and senior high levels. Teachers had strict requirements for the layout of drawings and the connection of lines.

Internships in the civil engineering department mainly consisted of surveying and construction internships. Surveying internships were divided into plane surveying and geodetic surveying. Plane surveying was usually conducted on campus or in nearby areas, while geodetic surveying often took place in Hangzhou, Wuxi, and other locations with different terrains and topography for surveying training. Construction internships usually involved teachers assigning engineering projects for students to practice designing. Sometimes, the school accepted construction design and supervision tasks from external units, and students would participate in actual work under the guidance of teachers to gain practical experience.

（4）商科 Business Department

商科的基本技能是小楷、珠算、打字和簿记。教师教学非常认真，经常采用勤学多练、从严要求的办法，使学生的基本技能达到较高的水平。

珠算是最重要的基本技能，除正课外，课外则加强练习，限时交卷。练习中还有听算法和速算法。五年不间断练习，要求学生将算盘打得滚瓜烂熟。

簿记练习在簿记教室进行，学生根据练习题独立做账，在规定时间内完成。练习所用簿册，要求学生自行画制。

shāng kē jiào shī hái jīng cháng zǔ zhī xué shēng dào yǒu guān dān wèi jìn xíng shí dì cān guān　diào
商科教师还经常组织学生到有关单位进行实地参观、调

chá hé shí xí　 shí xí shēng dà bù fen pài wǎng yín háng　 bǎo xiǎn gōng sī hé sān yǒu shí yè
查和实习，实习生大部分派往银行、保险公司和三友实业

shè　 zhāng huá máo fǎng chǎng děng gōng shāng yè dān wèi
社、章华毛纺厂等工商业单位。

The basic skills in the business department were calligraphy, abacus calculation, typing, and bookkeeping. Teachers were very serious in their teaching, often adopting methods of diligent practice and strict requirements to ensure that students' basic skills reached a high level.

Abacus calculation was the most important basic skill. In addition to regular classes, students practiced extensively outside of class and were required to submit their work within a time limit. The practice also included listening to calculation methods and speed calculation. Through five years of continuous practice, students were expected to become highly proficient in using the abacus.

Bookkeeping practice took place in the bookkeeping classroom, where students independently worked on accounting tasks based on practice questions and completed them within a specified time. The books used for practice were required to be drawn by the students themselves.

Business department teachers also regularly organized students to visit relevant units for on—site observation, investigation, and internships. Most interns were sent to banks, insurance companies, Sanyou Factory, Zhanghua Wool Factory, and other industrial and commercial enterprises.

6）校训 School Motto

“敬业乐群”，出自《礼记·学记》：“古之教者，家有塾，党有庠，术有序，国有学。比年入学，中年考校。一年视离经辨志，三年视敬业乐群，五年视博习亲师，七年视论学取友，谓之小成。”“敬业”指对所习之职业具有嗜好心，所在之事具责任心；“乐群”指具有优美和乐之情操及共同协作之精神。
jìng yè lè qún chū zì lǐ jì xué jì gǔ zhī jiào zhě jiā yǒu
shú dǎng yǒu xiáng shù yǒu xù guó yǒu xué bǐ nián rù xué zhōng nián kǎo jiào yī
nián shì lí jīng biàn zhì sān nián shì jìng yè lè qún wǔ nián shì bó xí qīn shī qī nián
shì lùn xué qǔ yǒu wèi zhī xiǎo chéng jìng yè zhǐ duì suǒ xí zhī zhí yè jù yǒu shì
hào xīn suǒ zài zhī shì jù zé rèn xīn lè qún zhǐ jù yǒu yōu měi hé lè zhī qíng cāo
jí gòng tóng xié zuò zhī jīng shén

The original Chinese version of “Respecting your profession and enjoying the community” originates from The Book of *Rites: The Record of Education*(《礼记·学记》), in which it literally means: “In ancient times, for education, families had private tutors, villages had local schools, districts had higher schools, and the nation had academies. Students entered school at a young age and were assessed in the middle years. After one year, they were evaluated on their understanding of the classics and their aspirations; after three years, on their respect for their profession and their enjoyment of community; after five years, on their extensive learning and close relationship with teachers; after seven years, on their ability to discuss knowledge and choose friends, which was considered a minor achievement”. “Respecting one's profession” refers to having a passion for the profession one is learning and the career one will pursue, and cultivating good professional interests and a sense of responsibility. "Enjoying the community" means having a refined and joyful temperament and a spirit of cooperation.

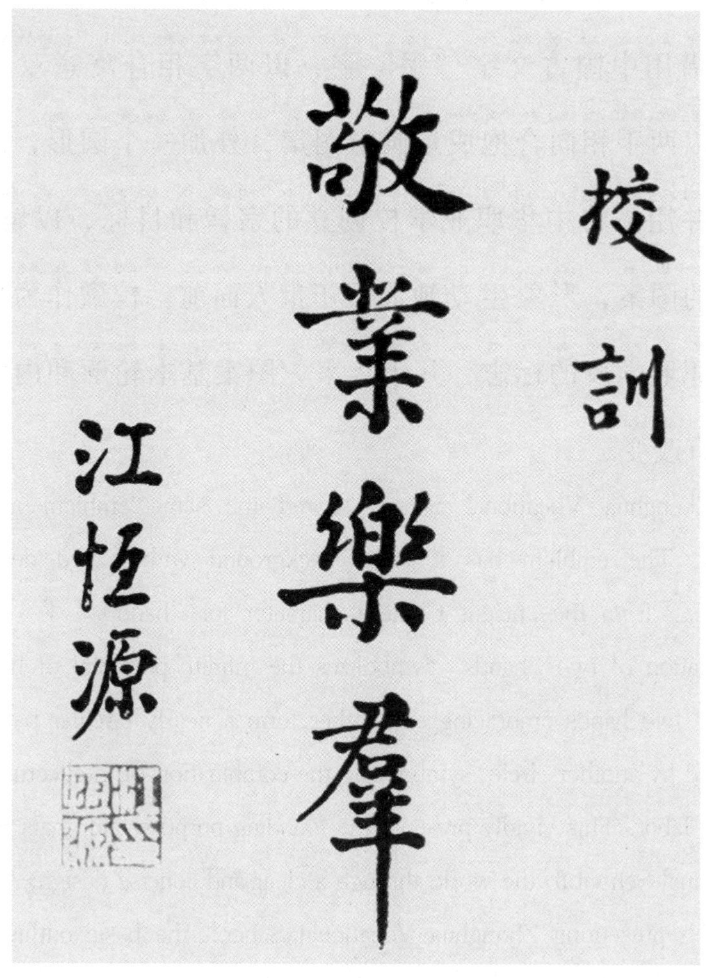

tú zhōng huá zhí yè xué xiào de xiào xùn
图3–9 中华职业学校的校训

Fig. 3 – 9 School motto of Zhonghua Vocational School

7）校徽 School Emblem

中华职业学校与中华职教社共享一校徽，图案白底红图，借用中国古文字“手”字，以两字相合寓意双手万能，以两手相向合抱成近圆形图案，外加一个圆形，寓意手脑并用，将中华职业学校创立的宗旨和目标，以鲜明、简练的图案，形象生动地展现于世人面前。校徽作为代表中华职业学校的标志，几十年来，图案基本轮廓和内涵一直没有改变。

Zhonghua Vocational School shared the same emblem as the CVEA. The emblem has a white background with a red design, borrowing from the ancient Chinese character for “hand” (手). The combination of two “hands” symbolizes the infinite potential of hands, and the two hands embracing each other form a nearly circular pattern, enclosed by another circle, symbolizing the combination of intellectual and manual labor. This vividly presents the founding purpose and goals of the Vocational School to the world through a clear and concise design. As the symbol representing Zhonghua Vocational School, the basic outline and connotation of the emblem have remained unchanged for decades.

tú zhōng huá zhí yè xué xiào de xiào huī
图3-10 中华职业学校的校徽

Fig. 3 – 10 School emblem of Zhonghua Vocational School

xiào zhāng
8）校章 School Badge

tú zhōng huá zhí yè xué xiào de xiào zhāng
图3–11　中华职业学校的校章

Fig. 3 – 11　School badge of Zhonghua Vocational School

xiào qí
9）校旗 School Flag

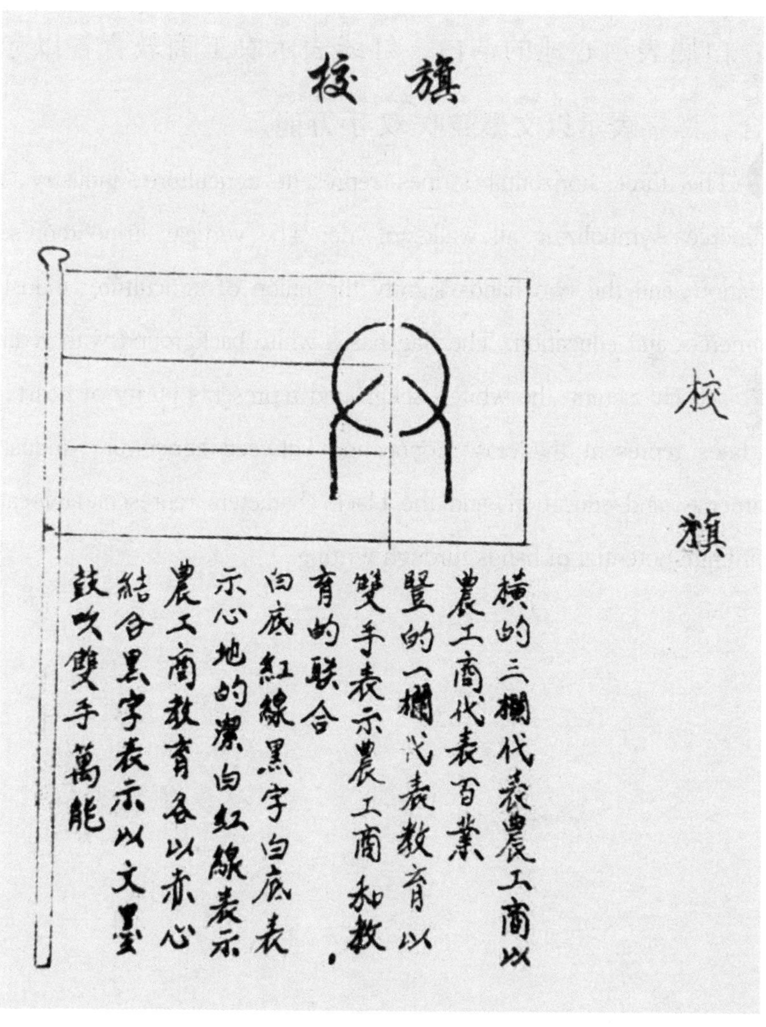

tú zhōng huá zhí yè xué xiào de xiào qí
图3–12 中华职业学校的校旗

Fig. 3 – 12 School flag of Zhonghua Vocational School

héng de sān lán dài biǎo nóng gōng shāng yǐ nóng gōng shāng dài biǎo bǎi yè shù dì yī lán
横的三栏代表农工商，以农工商代表百业，竖的一栏
dài biǎo jiào yù yǐ shuāng shǒu biǎo shì nóng gōng shāng hé jiào yù de lián hé bái dǐ hóng xiàn hēi
代表教育，以双手表示农工商和教育的联合，白底红线黑
zì bái dǐ biǎo shì xīn dì de jié bái hóng xiàn biǎo shì nóng gōng shāng jiào yù gè yǐ chì xīn
字：白底表示心地的洁白，红线表示农工商教育各以赤心
jié hé hēi zì biǎo shì yǐ wén mò gǔ chuī shuāng shǒu wàn néng
结合，黑字表示以文墨鼓吹双手万能。

The three horizontal stripes represent agriculture, industry, and commerce, symbolizing all walks of life. The vertical stripe represents education, and the two hands signify the union of agriculture, industry, commerce, and education. The flag has a white background with redlines and black characters: the white background represents purity of heart, the red lines represent the close connection between agriculture, industry, commerce, and education, and the black characters represent advocating the infinite potential of hands through writing.

xiào gē
10）校歌 School Song

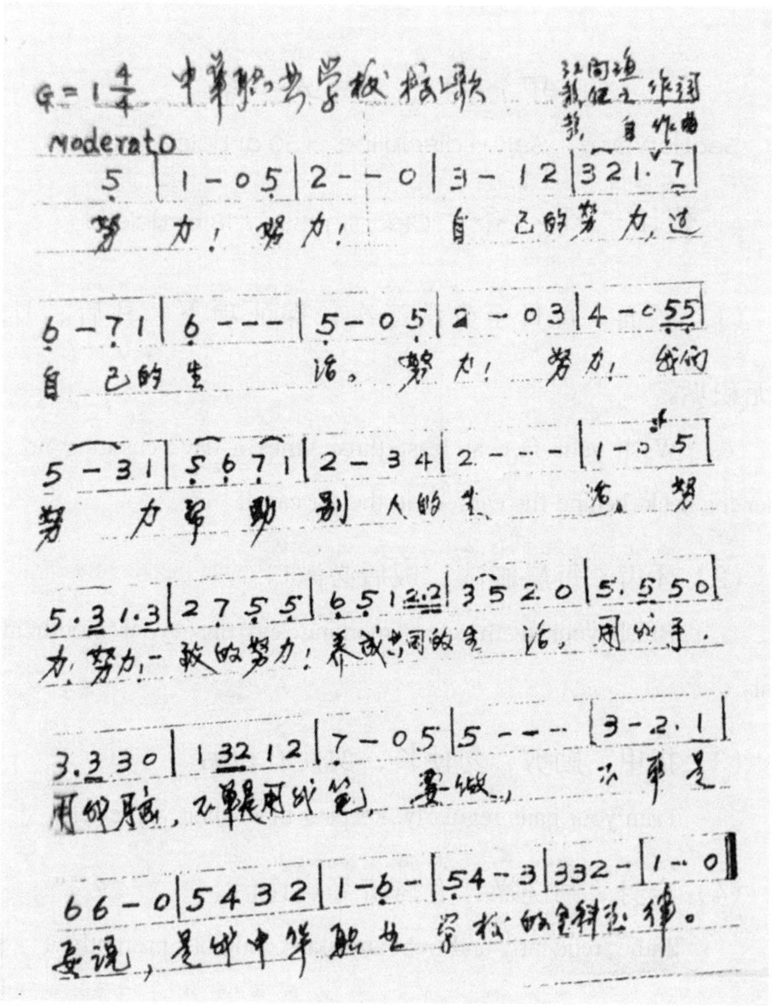

tú zhōng huá zhí yè xué xiào de xiào gē
图3–13 中华职业学校的校歌

Fig. 3 – 13 School song of Zhonghua Vocational School

zhōng huá zhí yè xué xiào xiū yǎng biāo zhǔn

11) 中华职业学校修养标准

Zhonghua Vocational School's Rules and Regulations

jiǎ   duì jǐ   gòng wǔ shí tiáo

（甲）对己　共五十条

Section One　Self－discipline　（50 articles in total）

zhěng jié   shí bā tiáo

整洁　十八条　Cleanliness　（18 articles）

yán miàn   měi rì zhì shǎo xǐ sān cì   bǎo zhèng xiàng xià   ěr hòu   ěr ké

（1）颜面　每日至少洗三次，保证项下、耳后、耳壳

chù wú jī gòu

处无积垢。

Wash your face at least three times a day, ensuring no dirt under the neck, behind the ears, or in the ear canal.

yá chǐ   měi chén shuā xǐ   fàn hòu bì shù kǒu

（2）牙齿　每晨刷洗，饭后必漱口。

Brush your teeth every morning and rinse your mouth after meals.

zhǐ jiǎ   qín jiǎn   wù shǐ zhǎng   wù shǐ yǒu jī gòu

（3）指甲　勤剪，勿使长，勿使有积垢。

Trim your nails regularly, keeping them short and clean.

quán shēn   qín xǐ zǎo   yǒu xuǎn jiè děng bìng sù zhì

（4）全身　勤洗澡，有癣疥等病速治。

Bathe frequently and treat any skin conditions promptly.

yī fu   nèi yī qín xǐ dí   wài yī pǔ sù yǎ jié   niǔ kòu yī lǜ kòu

（5）衣服　内衣勤洗涤；外衣朴素雅洁。纽扣一律扣

hǎo   yī wù yǒu zhàn liè sù bǔ   shōu cáng shí   dié fàng píng zhěng   wù shǐ shòu shī   wù

好，衣物有绽裂速补。收藏时，叠放平整，勿使受湿，勿

shǐ shēng chóng
使生虫。

Wash clothes and underwear regularly. Outerwear should be simple and elegant. Always fasten all buttons, and mend any tears or holes promptly. When storing clothes, fold them neatly, keep them dry, and prevent moths.

　　　　　mào　　　shì yàng jí yán sè xū wén yǎ dà fang　　dài shí lì qiú duān zhèng　　chú
（6）帽　式样及颜色需文雅大方，戴时力求端正。除
zài zì xiū shì jí qǐn shì wài　　bù dài zhē guāng mào jí yā fà mào
在自修室及寝室外，不戴遮光帽及压发帽。

Hats should be elegant in style and color, and worn properly. Do not wear hats that block the light or press on the hair, except in the study room or dormitory.

　　　　　wà　　qín xǐ　　wèi jí sǔn pò shí　　jí yù jiā bù dǐ　　shōu cáng yǒu dìng
（7）袜　勤洗，未及损破时，即预加布底，收藏有定
suǒ　　bù yǐ wū wà guà zhì yú rén suǒ yì jiàn zhī dì
所，不以污袜挂置于人所易见之地。

Wash socks frequently and add cloth to the soles before they wear out. Store them in a designated place and do not hang dirty socks in visible areas.

　　　　　xié　　qín shì　　qín shài　　xīn jiù huàn chuān　　shōu cáng yǒu dìng suǒ　　jué bù
（8）鞋　勤拭，勤晒，新旧换穿，收藏有定所，绝不
zòng héng zhì yú chuáng miàn zhī qián　　bù chuān yì fā dà shēng zhī mù jī
纵横置于床面之前。不穿易发大声之木屐。

Wipe and air shoes regularly, alternate between new and old pairs, and store them in a designated place. Never leave them scattered in front of the bed. Do not wear wooden clogs that make loud noises.

（9）被褥　勤洗，勤晒。每日起身后就寝前，各拂拭一次，不用时叠之使之雅观（并用白布一方覆于全床被褥之上，并挂下床面尺许）。

Wash and air bedding regularly. Dust them off every morning after getting up and before going to bed. When not in use, fold them neatly (and cover the entire bed with a white cloth, hanging down about a foot from the bed frame).

（10）床帐　帐内勿使有壁虱，如睡室内人多，每早起身后即撩起。

Do not allow bed bugs inside the bed curtains. If there are many people in the dormitory, lift the curtains every morning after getting up.

（11）面盆　面盆内外勤洗拭，不使有积垢，安放有定所，用时，勿使水溢于地。

Clean the washbasin inside and out regularly, ensuring it has no dirt. Place it in a designated spot, and do not spill water on the floor when using it.

（12）毛巾　用后挂置适当处所，勤用肥皂洗涤。

Hang towels in appropriate places after use and wash them frequently with soap.

xiāng lǒng ān fàng yú cáng xiāng shì nèi jì dōng shè èr jiān xī shè sān jiān rén gè yī gē yī cì ān zhì

（13）箱笼 安放于藏箱室内，计东舍二间，西舍三间，人各一格，依次安置。

Suitcases should be placed in the designated storage room. There are two rooms in the east wing and three rooms in the west wing, with one compartment for each person, arranged in order.

wǎn zhù chá hú chá bēi qín xǐ shì ān fàng yǒu dìng suǒ

（14）碗箸、茶壶、茶杯 勤洗拭，安放有定所。

Wash bowls, chopsticks, teapots, and teacups regularly and place them in designated spots.

shū zhuō qín fú shì zhuō biān zhuō tuǐ bìng xū zhù yì chōu ti nèi cún fàng gè wù yǒu zhì xù yǒu tiáo lǐ

（15）书桌 勤拂拭，桌边桌腿并须注意，抽屉内存放各物有秩序，有条理。

Wipe the desk regularly, paying attention to the edges and legs. Keep the drawers organized and tidy.

shū jí qín jiā shōu shí wù shǐ líng luàn shū miàn shū jiǎo shí shí liú yì bù shǐ wū sǔn juǎn qū

（16）书籍 勤加收拾，勿使凌乱，书面书角，时时留意，不使污损卷曲。

Organize books regularly, do not leave them messy. Pay attention to the covers and corners of books, preventing them from getting dirty or curled.

bǐ yàn bǐ yòng hòu jiā tào yàn yòng hòu jiā gài

（17）笔砚 笔用后加套，砚用后加盖。

Put covers on pens after use and lids oninkstones after use.

xìn jiàn yīng bǎo cún zhě jiǎn qí fàng zài yī qǐ

（18）信件 应保存者，检齐放在一起。

Keep letters that need to be saved together in one place.

wèi shēng shí liù tiáo
卫生 十六条 Hygiene （16 articles）

yī shí qǐ shuì
（19）依时起睡。

Rise and sleep on time.

xíng zǒu zuò lì shí tóu zhèng xiōng tǐng yāo zhí
（20）行走坐立时，头正胸挺腰直。

Walk, sit, and stand with your head held high, chest out, and back straight.

wú lùn hé dì jué bu suí yì tǔ tán
（21）无论何地，绝不随意吐痰。

Never spit indiscriminately, regardless of location.

yī rì sān cān gè yī dìng shí cǐ wài jué bù kě gòu mǎi zá shí
（22）一日三餐，各依定时，此外绝不可购买杂食。

Have three meals a day at regular times, and do not buy snacks in between.

fēi zhì wàn bù dé yǐ shí bù yòng kāi shuǐ táo fàn
（23）非至万不得已时，不用开水淘饭。

Do not rinse rice with boiling water unless absolutely necessary.

bù shí yǐ fǔ bài zhī ròu shū shuǐ guǒ
（24）不食已腐败之肉蔬水果。

Do not eat spoiled meat, vegetables, or fruits.

shí bù guò bǎo
（25）食不过饱。

Do not overeat.

shí shí jiā yì jǔ jué
（26）食时加意咀嚼。

Chew your food thoroughly.

fàn hòu kè qián huǎn bù tíng yuàn bù xíng jī liè yùn dòng
（27）饭后课前缓步庭院，不行激烈运动。

Take a slow walk in the courtyard after meals and before class, avoiding strenuous exercise.

yùn dòng yǒu héng
（28）运动有恒。

Exercise regularly.

yǒu xiǎo bìng cóng sù yǎng zhì
（29）有小病从速养治。

Seek prompt treatment for minor ailments.

rú huàn shāng fēng shā yǎn děng chuán rǎn bìng shí bù yòng gōng gòng shǒu jīn bìng zhù yì zì jǐ shǒu jīn de ān fàng
（30）如患伤风沙眼等传染病时，不用公共手巾，并注意自己手巾的安放。

If you have a contagious disease like a cold or pink eye, do not use shared towels and be mindful of where you place your own towel.

bù zài guāng xiàn hēi àn chù kàn shū gèng bù cáng zài zhàng nèi huò tǎng zài chuáng shàng kàn shū
（31）不在光线黑暗处看书，更不藏在帐内或躺在床上看书。

Do not read in dim light, and especially avoid reading under the covers or lying in bed.

dú shū shí shǒu lǐ de shū bù lí yǎn tài yuǎn
（32）读书时手里的书不离眼太远。

Keep the book at a reasonable distance from your eyes while reading.

xiě zì shí shēn tǐ bù guò fèn qián qīng miǎn shāng fèi bù
（33）写字时身体不过分前倾，免伤肺部。

Do not lean forward excessively while writing to avoid straining your lungs.

píng shí liú xīn wèi shēng zhī shi gòu mǎi jiǎn míng wèi shēng shū jí
（34）平时留心卫生知识，购买简明卫生书籍。

Pay attention to hygiene knowledge and purchase concise hygiene books.

láo dòng sì tiáo
劳动 四条 Labor （4 articles）

zì jǐ shì zì jǐ zuò fēi zhì wàn bù dé yǐ bù hū huàn xiào gōng
（35）自己事，自己做，非至万不得已，不呼唤校工。

Do your own chores and do not call for school staff unless absolutely necessary.

rèn dìng shǒu nǎo bìng yòng shì zuò rén de běn fèn
（36）认定手脑并用是做人的本分。

Recognize that combining intellectual and manual labor is a fundamental part of being a person.

yǐ láo dòng wéi lè yǐ ān xián xiū xi wéi kǔ
（37）以劳动为乐，以安闲休息为苦。

Find joy in labor and shame in idleness.

fán sǎo dì shì zhuō děng guān yú gōng gòng lì yì zhī shì suī yì dìng lún zhí zài běn rén fāng miàn yīng gāi yuàn yì duō zuò bìng qiě néng qiè shí zuò qù bù xū jiào shī jiān chá
（38）凡扫地拭桌等关于公共利益之事，虽议定轮值，在本人方面，应该愿意多做，并且能切实做去，不须教师监察。

Regarding tasks that benefit the public, such as sweeping the floor and wiping tables, even if there is a rotation schedule, be willing to do more and do it thoroughly without the need for teacher supervision.

jié jiǎn shí èr tiáo
节俭 十二条 Thrift（12 articles）

suí shēn líng yòng qián cún fàng zài shì dàng chù suǒ
（39）随身零用钱存放在适当处所。

Keep your pocket money in a designated place.

shè lì bù jì fēn bié shōu zhī suí shí jì zǎi jué bù jiàn duàn
（40）设立簿记，分别收支，随时记载，绝不间断。

Maintain a record of income and expenses, recording them regularly without interruption.

yuè zhōng jiāng shōu zhī yòng kuǎn xiáng xì bào gào jiā zhǎng
（41）月中将收支用款详细报告家长。

Provide a detailed report of income and expenses to your parents in the middle of the month.

bù gòu wú yòng de wán hǎo pǐn jí xiāo fèi wù
（42）不购无用的玩好品及消费物。

Do not buy useless toys or luxury items.

duì yú zì jǐ de bǐ mò zhǐ shū jiā yǐ ài xī jué bù làng fèi
（43）对于自己的笔墨纸书，加以爱惜，绝不浪费。

Cherish your pens, ink, paper, and books, and never waste them.

bù rǎn bù liáng de shì hào
（44）不染不良的嗜好。

Do not indulge in bad habits.

bù rù wú yì de yú lè chǎng
（45）不入无益的娱乐场。

Do not participate in useless entertainment.

yòng qián shí xiān sī liang dào lái zhī bù yì jì suàn shōu yì jǐ hé
（46）用钱时先思量到来之不易，计算收益几何。

Before spending money, think about how hard it is to earn and calculate the benefits.

qián néng zhī pèi dé fǎ
（47）钱能支配得法。

Manage your money wisely.

shí xíng chǔ xù
（48）实行储蓄。

Practice saving.

jié shěng shí jiān
（49）节省时间。

Save time.

gōng zuò shí néng yòng zuì jīng jì de fāng fǎ, miǎn jīng jì jí shí jiān zhī xū hào
（50）工作时能用最经济的方法，免经济及时间之虚耗。

Use the most economical methods when working to avoid wasting money and time.

yǐ duì rén gòng wǔ shí sì tiáo
（乙）对人　共五十四条

Section Two　Interpersonal Relations （54 articles in total）

duì shī zhǎng shí tiáo
对师长　十条　To Teachers （10 articles）

shí shí cún zūn zhòng xīn jí jìng ài xīn
（51）时时存尊重心及敬爱心。

Always maintain respect and love for teachers.

wú lùn zài xiào nèi xiào wài, měi rì dì yī cì jiàn miàn, bì jū gōng wèn hǎo
（52）无论在校内校外，每日第一次见面，必鞠躬问好。

Whether on or off campus, bow and greet teachers the first time you see them each day.

shàng kè bù chí dào zǎo tuì wú gù bù quē xí
（53）上课不迟到早退，无故不缺席。

Do not be late for class, leave early, or be absent without reason.

xiān sheng dào jiào shì shàng kè shí qǐ lì wéi lǐ
（54）先生到教室上课时，起立为礼。

Stand up as a sign of respect when the teacher enters the classroom.

zài shàng kè shí rú yù fā wèn bì xiān jǔ shǒu dé jiào shī yǔn kě rán hòu fā wèn wèn shí tài dù qiān hé
（55）在上课时，如欲发问，必先举手，得教师允可，然后发问，问时态度谦和。

If you want to ask a question during class, raise your hand first, wait for the teacher's permission, and then ask politely.

shī zhǎng yǒu wèn jù shí chén bào bù jiā yǐn shì
（56）师长有问，据实陈报，不加隐饰。

Answer truthfully and without concealment when asked by teachers.

shuō huà píng hé qīng lǎng
（57）说话平和清朗。

Speak calmly and clearly.

shòu xiān sheng jiào xùn néng fú cóng bìng zhī gǎn jī
（58）受先生教训，能服从，并知感激。

Obey the teacher's instructions and be grateful.

shī zhǎng yǒu bù kuài yì shì qīn dào huò xiě xìn qù ān wèi
（59）师长有不快意事，亲到或写信去安慰。

If a teacher seems disheartened, visit or write to them to offer comfort.

shī zhǎng yǒu suǒ zhǐ shì lì shǐ shàng yǒu míng rén wù jí jìn shì chéng gōng de shì yè jiā bì xì xīn kǎo jiu qí yán xíng shù lì wéi zì shēn xíng wéi de mó fàn

（60）师长有所指示历史上有名人物及近世成功的事业家，必细心考究其言行，树立为自身行为的模范。

Carefully study the words and deeds of historical figures and successful entrepreneurs mentioned by teachers, and take them as role models for your own behavior.

duì tóng xué jí tóng bèi èr shí liù tiáo

对同学及同辈　二十六条

To Classmates and Peers （26 articles）

shí shí cún yǒu ài xīn

（61）时时存友爱心。

Always have a heart of friendship.

shí shí bǎo chí qiān hé tài dù

（62）时时保持谦和态度。

Always maintain a humble and polite attitude.

jiàn miàn yǒu lǐ mào

（63）见面有礼貌。

Greet others politely.

shuō huà shí tài du chéng kěn

（64）说话时态度诚恳。

Be sincere when speaking.

duì nián zhǎng tóng xué jìng zhòng duì nián yòu tóng xué ài hù

（65）对年长同学敬重，对年幼同学爱护。

Respect older classmates and care for younger ones.

bù kuā jǐ cháng bù xiào rén duǎn
（66）不夸己长，不笑人短。

Do not boast about your strengths or laugh at others' shortcomings.

bù yǐ kē kè yǔ jiā rén
（67）不以苛刻语加人。

Do not speak harshly to others.

bù bèi hòu yì rén cháng duǎn
（68）不背后议人长短。

Do not gossip about others behind their backs.

nán nǚ jiāo jì tài dù dà fang
（69）男女交际，态度大方。

Interact with the opposite sex in a generous and appropriate manner.

yù rù yǒu rén zhī shì hū yìng hòu zài rù
（70）欲入友人之室，呼应后再入。

When entering someone's room, knock and wait for a response before entering.

bù xiè lòu bié rén de mì mì
（71）不泄露别人的秘密。

Do not divulge others' secrets.

rén ruò yǒu shì shí jué bù gāo shēng tán xiào huò yǐ wú guān zhòng yào zhī yán zǔ qí jìn xíng
（72）人若有事时，绝不高声谈笑，或以无关重要之言，阻其进行。

Do not talk or laugh loudly when others are busy, or interrupt their progress with unimportant matters.

tóng xué yǒu yí shì lái wèn jiù jǐ suǒ zhī xiáng xì yǐ gào
（73）同学有疑事来问，就己所知，详细以告。

If a classmate asks you a question, answer them in detail to the best of your knowledge.

tóng xué yǒu kùn nan shì qiú zhù zì liàng lì néng wéi zhù zé jié lì zhù zhī bù néng wéi zhù zé hé yán wǎn cí yǐ xiè zhī
(74) 同学有困难事求助，自量力能为助，则竭力助之；不能为助，则和颜婉辞以谢之。

If a classmate asks for help with something difficult, do your best to help them. If you cannot help, politely decline.

tóng xué jiān yǒu zhēng yì jié lì wèi zhī pái jiě
(75) 同学间有争议，竭力为之排解。

Try your best to mediate disputes between classmates.

duì tóng xué bù jí jì bù jì qián chóu
(76) 对同学不嫉忌，不记前仇。

Do not be jealous of or hold grudges against classmates.

duì tóng xué jiān bù cún fēn pài xīn lǐ
(77) 对同学间不存分派心理。

Do not form cliques among classmates.

bié rén chéng gōng wǒ yě kuài lè
(78) 别人成功，我也快乐。

Be happy for others' successes.

bié rén yǒu tòng kǔ wǒ yě gǎn dào bù kuài
(79) 别人有痛苦，我也感到不快。

Feel empathy for others' pain.

tóng xué yǒu bù chèn xīn de shì gǎn kuài qù ān wèi
(80) 同学有不称心的事，赶快去安慰。

Offer comfort to classmates who are feeling down.

yǔ yǒu jiāo jiē bù yīn xiǎo shì dòu yì qì
(81) 与友交接，不因小事斗意气。

Do not engage in petty arguments with friends.

bù yǔ tóng xué suí yì xì xuè
（82）不与同学随意戏谑。

Do not engage in frivolous banter with classmates.

yǔ rén jiā shuō xiào hua bù shè qīng tiāo cū bǐ
（83）与人家说笑话，不涉轻佻粗鄙。

Avoid being flippant or vulgar when telling jokes.

yùn dòng bǐ sài shí duì yú duì fāng yǒu lǐ mào jué bù yīn shèng ér jiāo yīn bài ér nù
（84）运动比赛时，对于对方有礼貌，绝不因胜而骄，因败而怒。

Be polite to opponents during sports competitions and never be arrogant in victory orangry in defeat.

biàn lùn wèn tí shí tài du wēn hé yán yǔ míng xī bù jí qiè bù zá luàn bù yǐ shèng qì líng rén
（85）辩论问题时，态度温和，言语明晰，不急切，不杂乱，不以盛气凌人。

During debates, maintain a calm demeanor, speak clearly, and avoid being hasty, disorganized, or condescending.

tóng xué yǒu bù zhèng dāng de jǔ dòng wǎn yán jiàn zǔ huò shè fǎ shì yì shǐ zhī kuì wù
（86）同学有不正当的举动，婉言谏阻，或设法示意使之愧悟。

If a classmate behaves inappropriately, gently admonish them or find ways to make them realize their mistake.

duì jiào gōng liù tiáo
对校工 六条 To School Staff （6 articles）

shí shí cún píng děng dài yù de guān niàn
（87）时时存平等待遇的观念。

Always treat them with equality.

yǒu jī huì shī yǐ bǔ xí jiào yù
（88）有机会施以补习教育。

Offer supplementary education when possible.

zūn zhòng xiào gōng zhí xíng zhī zhí wù jué bù yǔ zhī wéi nán
（89）尊重校工执行之职务，绝不与之为难。

Respect the duties of the school staff and never make things difficult for them.

bù suí yì hū huàn xiào gōng
（90）不随意呼唤校工。

Do not summon school staff unnecessarily.

bù sī gěi wù zhì zhī chóu bào xiàn rén yú bù yì
（91）不私给物质之酬报，陷人于不义。

Do not offer material rewards in private, leading them into wrongdoing.

wú shì shí bù zài xiào gōng shì nèi dòu liú
（92）无事时不在校工室内逗留。

Do not linger in the staff room when you have nothing to do.

duì qún shí èr tiáo
对群　十二条　To the Community （12 Articles）

kāi huì shí jué bù wú gù quē xí bìng néng yī shí jìn tuì
（93）开会时绝不无故缺席，并能依时进退。

Never be absent from meetings without good reason, and arrive and leave on time.

yán shǒu gōng gòng zhì xù
（94）严守公共秩序。

Strictly observe public order.

huì shí shí yǒu lǐ mào
（95）会食时有礼貌。

Be polite during meals.

jí huì jù cān shí bù suí yì gāo shēng jiǎng huà
（96）集会聚餐时，不随意高声讲话。

Do not talk loudly at gatherings or dinners.

cān jiā huì yì shí duì yú gè yì àn néng xì xīn yán jiū jǐ yǒu yì jiàn néng jǐn liàng fā biǎo àn jīng duō shù yì jué jí biǎo shì fú cóng bù jiān chí jǐ jiàn
（97）参加会议时，对于各议案，能细心研究，己有意见，能尽量发表，案经多数议决，即表示服从，不坚持己见。

When participating in meetings, carefully study each proposal, express your opinions if you have any, and show obedience to the majority decision without insisting on your own views.

fú cóng shǒu lǐng zhǐ huī
（98）服从首领指挥。

Obey the leader's commands.

jìn lì wèi tuán tǐ fú wù
（99）尽力为团体服务。

Do your best to serve the community.

shí shí cún ài hù tuán tǐ de guān niàn
（100）时时存爱护团体的观念。

Always cherish the community.

shí shí cún fā dá tuán tǐ de guān niàn
（101）时时存发达团体的观念。

Always strive to develop the community.

shí shí shè fǎ gǎi jìn tuán tǐ shēng huó wèi gōng zhòng móu fú lì
（102）时时设法改进团体生活，为公众谋福利。

Always seek ways to improve community life and promote public welfare.

néng zhī dào guó chǐ shí shí cún xuě chǐ xīn
（103）能知道国耻，时时存雪耻心。

Be aware of national humiliation and always strive to redeem it.

rèn dìng rè ài guó jiā shì guó mín wéi yī de tiān zhí
（104）认定热爱国家是国民唯一的天职。

Recognize that loving the country is the sole duty of every citizen.

bǐng duì wù gòng shí bā tiáo
（丙）对物 共十八条

Section Three Respect for Property （18 articles in total）

jǐ wù sān tiáo
己物 三条 Personal Belongings （3 articles）

tè bié ài xī suī zhì fèi qì réng sī shè fǎ lì yòng
（105）特别爱惜，虽至废弃，仍思设法利用。

Cherish your belongings and, even when they are no longer needed, consider ways to repurpose them.

jǐ wù yǒu yú yǒu wù quē zhī jǐn kě zhuó liang fēn zèng
（106）己物有余，友物缺之，尽可酌量分赠。

If you have surplus items and your friends lack them, share them appropriately.

líng xīng gè wù jì rù bù nèi yǐ miǎn yí wàng
（107）零星各物，计入簿内，以免遗忘。

Keep a record of small items to avoid forgetting them.

yǒu wù qī tiáo
友物 七条 Friends' Belongings (7 articles)

tè bié zūn zhòng, rú wèi qián cái líng wù, yǒu bù zài shì, jué bù xiāng jìn
(108) 特别尊重，如为钱财零物，友不在室，绝不相近。

Show special respect for friends' belongings, especially money and small items. Do not go near them when your friends are not present.

fēi zhì wàn bù dé yǐ, bù xiàng yǒu rén jiè wù
(109) 非至万不得已，不向友人借物。

Do not borrow from friends unless absolutely necessary.

yǒu rén sī xìn bù chāi kàn
(110) 友人私信不拆看。

Do not open friends' private letters.

yǒu rén kàn sī xìn shí, jǐ bì lí kāi
(111) 友人看私信时，己必离开。

Leave when a friend is reading private letters.

yù qǔ yǒu rén shū wù kàn, xū xiān shāng dé tóng yì, kàn hòu jiāo huán shí, bìng xū biǎo shì xiè yì
(112) 欲取友人书物看，须先商得同意，看后交还时，并须表示谢意。

Ask for permission before borrowing a friend's books or belongings, and express gratitude when returning them.

shòu rén zèng yī wù, bì yǒu yǐ bào, dàn xū liáng yī jǐ zhī cái lì xíng zhī, chāo guò yī dìng xiàn dù, bì bào gào jiā zhǎng, suǒ bào zhī wù, dàn lì qiú qí hé yú shí yòng
(113) 受人赠衣物，必有以报，但须量一己之财力行之，超过一定限度，必报告家长，所报之物，但力求其合于实用。

Reciprocate gifts of clothing or items, but within your

financial means. If exceeding a certain limit, inform your parents, and choose gifts that are practical.

（114）友人与己以不义之物，详审是非利害，婉言拒绝。

If a friend offers you something inappropriate, carefully consider the right and wrong, the pros and cons, and politely decline.

公物　八条　Public Property （8 articles）

（115）不折花木。

Do not damage flowers or trees.

（116）不污庭院墙壁。

Do not deface courtyards or walls.

（117）爱护公物，胜于己物，绝不任意毁坏，即偶不经心毁坏公物时，亦必直认赔偿。

Cherish public property more than your own, never intentionally damage it. If you accidentally damage public property, admit it and compensate for it.

（118）保管公物，郑重审慎，记载详明，一丝不苟。

Be cautious and meticulous when managing public property, keep detailed records, and be meticulous.

dài gòu gōng wù rú gòu jǐ wù yī yàng xiáng chá jià mù bù shè hán hu
（119）代购公物，如购己物一样，详查价目，不涉含糊。

When purchasing public property on behalf of others, be as careful as when purchasing for yourself, check prices carefully, and avoid ambiguity.

rú yù tè bié qíng xing gōng sī liǎng wù bù néng liǎng quán shí bì shě jǐ wù ér quán gōng wù
（120）如遇特别情形，公私两物不能两全时，必舍己物而全公物。

In special circumstances, when public and private interests cannot be reconciled, sacrifice personal belongings to protect public property.

gōng wù jiāng bèi huǐ yóu jǐ bǎo hù zhī bù shǐ shòu sǔn rèn dìng cǐ shì wéi zuò rén yào dào kě yǐ bó dé liáng xīn shàng zhī ān wèi
（121）公物将被毁，由己保护之，不使受损；认定此事为做人要道，可以博得良心上之安慰。

Protect public property from damage and consider it a fundamental principle of being a person, gaining peace of conscience.

rèn dìng qīn shí gōng zhòng yī qián sǔn huǐ gōng zhòng yī wù wéi yī shēng mò dà chǐ rǔ liáng xīn jiāng yǔ yǐ wú qióng tòng kǔ
（122）认定侵蚀公众一钱，损毁公众一物，为一生莫大耻辱，良心将予以无穷痛苦。

Consider misappropriating public funds or damaging public property as the greatestshame in life, causing endless suffering to one's conscience.

dīng duì shì gòng èr shí bā tiáo
（丁）对事　共二十八条

Section Four　Conduct in Affairs（28 articles in total）

měi zuò yī jiàn shì chū yī yán bì xiān jiā yǐ zhèng zhòng de kǎo lǜ
（123）每做一件事，出一言，必先加以郑重的考虑。

Think carefully before taking any action or speaking any word.

duì yú páng rén suǒ zuò de shì suǒ tán de shì néng suí shí liú xīn
（124）对于旁人所做的事，所谈的事，能随时留心。

Pay attention to what others are doing and talking about.

měi rì yīng zuò zhī shì yīng cóng róng bù pò àn cì zuò wán
（125）每日应做之事，应从容不迫，按次做完。

Complete daily tasks in composure and in order.

běn rì néng zuò wán zhī shì jué bù liú dài míng rì
（126）本日能做完之事，绝不留待明日。

Do not procrastinate; finish today's tasks today.

zuò shì néng hé zuò rén hé zuò
（127）做事能和做人合作。

Cooperate with others in work and life.

huān xǐ hé bié rén yī tóng zuò shì
（128）欢喜和别人一同做事。

Enjoy working with others.

lì dìng zhì yuàn shǐ jīn rì zuò de shì yī dìng bǐ zuó rì zuò dé hǎo
（129）立定志愿，使今日做的事，一定比昨日做得好。

Set goals to make today's work better than yesterday's.

měi wǎn rù qǐn shì shí néng fǎn xǐng yī rì jiān suǒ yán suǒ xíng hé zhě wéi shì hé zhě wéi fēi
（130）每晚入寝室时，能反省一日间所言所行，何者为是，何者为非。

Reflect on your words and actions each night before bed, discerning right from wrong.

xiǎo shàn xiǎo è jiē néng tè bié zhù yì
（131）小善小恶，皆能特别注意。

Pay special attention to even small acts of kindness or evil.

zì jǐ zuò cuò de shì néng bù jiā yǎn shì néng yǒng yú huǐ gǎi
（132）自己做错的事，能不加掩饰，能勇于悔改。

Admit your mistakes without concealment and have the courage to repent.

rèn dìng mù xū róng wéi zuì kě wù de xīn lǐ
（133）认定慕虚荣为最可恶的心理。

Recognize vanity as the most despicable mentality.

lìng rén bù yú kuài de jǔ dòng néng zhù yì bì miǎn
（134）令人不愉快的举动，能注意避免。

Avoid actions that displease others.

rén yǒu fēi lǐ jiā wǒ bù wéi guò fèn de fǎn dòng
（135）人有非礼加我，不为过分的反动。

Do not overreact to others' disrespectful behavior towards you.

rén jiā yǒu wú xīn de guò shī néng jiā yǐ yuán liàng
（136）人家有无心的过失，能加以原谅。

Forgive others' unintentional mistakes.

rén jiā qiú wǒ de shì néng xiáng jiā kǎo lǜ jué dìng kě fǒu ér hòu zài biǎo shì
（137）人家求我的事，能详加考虑，决定可否，而后再表示。

Carefully consider requests from others and express your decision after determining whether it is feasible.

yǐ dā ying bié rén zuò de shì lì kè jiù qù jìn lì zuò
（138）已答应别人做的事，立刻就去尽力做。

Immediately do your best to fulfill promises made to others.

zuò shì néng rěn nài
（139）做事能忍耐。

Be patient when doing things.

lùn shì shí duì yú shì de nèi róng jí jīng guò bù míng liǎo jué bù wàng jiā pī píng
（140）论事时对于事的内容及经过不明了，绝不妄加批评。

Do not criticize blindly without understanding the content and process of a matter.

lùn shì shí néng tì dāng shì rén shè shēn chǔ dì qù xiǎng
（141）论事时能替当事人设身处地去想。

Put yourself in the shoes of others when discussing matters.

yǎn shù yī shì bù xíng róng tài guò shǐ zhī shī zhēn
（142）演述一事，不形容太过，使之失真。

Do not exaggerate when recounting events, so as not to distort the truth.

chǔ lǐ gōng jia shì yào yǐ dà duō shù rén de lì yì wéi qián tí yǒu shí nìng kě xī shēng xiǎo jǐ yǐ quán dà zhòng
（143）处理公家事，要以大多数人的利益为前提，有时宁可牺牲小己，以全大众。

When handling public affairs, prioritize the interests of the majority, sometimes sacrificing personal interests for the greater good.

guān yú ài hù guó jiā de shì bù yīng luò hòu
（144）关于爱护国家的事，不应落后。

Do not lag in matters concerning the protection of the country.

（145）遇有困难事，要亟待解决时，能先用冷静的头脑，想明来源去路，然后再拟好步骤，按定办理，用和平手段，坚毅心志，勇敢气概，一步一步向前去做。

When encountering difficulties that require urgent solutions, first use a calm mind to think clearly about the cause and effect, then formulate a plan, and proceed stepby step with peaceful means, determination, and courage.

（146）做事方法不同，能随地随时明晰思考，运用以往经验，一面做，一面学。

When faced with different working methods, think clearly, apply past experiences, and learn while doing.

（147）无论何事，做起来皆抱有快乐的态度。

Maintain a joyful attitude in all endeavors.

（148）做事论事，皆精密有条理。

Be meticulous and organized in work and discussions.

（149）做事论事，皆能先寻着扼要之处。

Identify the key points when working or discussing matters.

（150）做事论事，皆能重用理性，不枉逞感情。

Rely on reason, not emotions, when working or discussing matters.

wù duì xué wèn zhī shi gòng èr shí tiáo
（戊）对学问知识　共二十条

Section Five　Knowledge and Learning（20 articles in total）

xiān sheng jiǎng jiě, jìng xīn tīng shòu
（151）先生讲解，静心听受。

Listen attentively to the teacher's instructions.

yǒu xū yù xí zhī gōng kè, néng chōng fèn yù xí
（152）有须预习之功课，能充分预习。

Prepare thoroughly for lessons that require previewing.

chū jiào shì hòu, néng àn shí wēn xí gōng kè
（153）出教室后，能按时温习功课。

Review lessons promptly after leaving the classroom.

gōng kè yǒu bù liǎo jiě de, néng lì qiú liǎo jiě, rú ruò zì jǐ yǐ jīng guò yī fān sī suǒ kǎo lǜ hòu, réng bù liǎo jiě, zé zài qǐng wèn tóng xué huò shī zhǎng
（154）功课有不了解的，能力求了解，如若自己已经过一番思索考虑后，仍不了解，则再请问同学或师长。

If you don't understand something, strive to understand it. If you still don't understand after careful consideration, ask your classmates or teachers for help.

rèn dìng chāo xí bié rén gōng kè, shì yī jiàn jí wéi kě chǐ de shì
（155）认定抄袭别人功课，是一件极为可耻的事。

Recognize that copying others' work is shameful.

kè wài zhǒng zhǒng huó dòng, jiē néng yǒu yì yú shēn xīn
（156）课外种种活动，皆能有益于身心。

Participate in extracurricular activities that benefit both body and mind.

（157）到假期时，能将假期内预备自修之功课，先行拟定，并能按照原定计划，切实自修，假满入校，应向先生报告。

Plan your self—study schedule for vacations in advance and follow it diligently. Report your progress to the teacher upon returning to school.

（158）勤笔记，不间断。

Take notes diligently and consistently.

（159）读完一部书或一篇文章，能深入思考，必求明了其意义而后已。

After reading a book or an article, think deeply about it and strive to understand its meaning.

（160）作文不苟且。

Do not be careless in writing.

（161）能时时留察自己的个性，宜于何项功课，不宜于何项功课。

Be aware of your strengths and weaknesses in different subjects.

（162）自己喜欢研究的功课，能不断地努力研究。

Continuously strive to study the subjects you enjoy.

（163）自己不喜欢的功课，如认定与自己一生做人及将来做事有关，亦能特别努力，求达到水平线以上的程度。

Even if you dislike a subject, if you recognize its relevance to your life and future career, make an extra effort to achieve above-average proficiency.

（164）能认定自己将来操何项职业，即努力从事何项功课。

Identify your future career path and diligently pursue the relevant studies.

（165）时时留心职业界的现状，并加以调查记载。

Pay attention to the current situation in the professional world and conduct research and record your findings.

（166）能于教室功课以外，留心多阅读关于职业及有关个人修养之书籍。至于读何书为最宜，则先请教师指导。

In addition to classroom studies, read extensively about your chosen profession and personal development. Consult your teachers for guidance on book selection.

（167）能常就校内所信仰的先生，讨论个人将来职业问题，以预为之备。

Regularly discuss your future career plans with trusted teachers at school to prepare in advance.

yù bèi guān yú zhí yè gōng kè shí bìng néng shí shí jiān gù dào rén gé de xiū yǎng
（168）预备关于职业功课时，并能时时兼顾到人格的修养。

While preparing for your professional studies, always consider the cultivation of your character.

shí shí móu xīn zhī shi de shū rù hé xīn jīng yàn de kuò chōng
（169）时时谋新知识的输入和新经验的扩充。

Continuously seek new knowledge and expand your experiences.

měi rì bù duàn de yuè dú bào zhǐ duì yú guó jiā shè huì yǒu guān de shì yào tè bié liú xīn
（170）每日不断地阅读报纸，对于国家社会有关的事，要特别留心。

Read newspapers daily and pay special attention to matters concerning the nation and society.

zì xǐng shí liù zé
12）自省（十六则）Self–Examination （16 rules）

wǒ de tuǐ néng yī tiān pǎo bā jiǔ shí lǐ bù gǎn jiào pí láo me
（1）我的腿，能一天跑八九十里，不感觉疲劳么？

Can I run 40 or 50 kilometers a day without fatigue?

wǒ de bì hé shǒu néng ná yī bǎi duō jīn de dōng xi jīng guò jiào cháng shí jiān bù jué de kǔ me
（2）我的臂和手，能拿一百多斤的东西，经过较长时间，不觉得苦么？

Can I carry over 100 pounds for an extended period without

feeling strained?

（3）我的肚皮，能经过十小时，不吃饭，不饮水，照常工作么？

Can I work for ten hours without food or water?

（4）我的嘴，能发很有条理的言语么？

Can I speak logically and coherently?

（5）我的态度，能很端正，很谦和么？

Can I maintain an upright and humble posture?

（6）我的脑和手，联合起来，能写成词能达意的文字么？

Can my mind and hands work together to write meaningful words?

（7）我的注意力，能不遗漏较小的事情么？

Can I pay attention to even the smallest details?

（8）我的心思，能时时刻刻向好处去想，向好处去求么？

Do I consistently direct my thoughts towards positive outcomes?

（9）我的理智，能指挥我的情感，节制我的冲动么？

Can I control my emotions and impulses with reason?

wǒ néng zì zhī wǒ de duǎn chù lì móu gǎi shàn me
（10）我能自知我的短处，力谋改善么？

Can I recognize my shortcomings and strive to improve?

wǒ néng gòu tīng wǒ shī cháng hé péng you guī quàn de huà bù dòng qì ér qiě gǎn jī me
（11）我能够听我师长和朋友规劝的话，不动气而且感激么？

Can I listen to advice from mentors and friends without anger and with gratitude?

wǒ duì yú wǒ de péng you shuō huà néng bù shī xìn me
（12）我对于我的朋友，说话能不失信么？

Can I keep my word to my friends?

wǒ suǒ yòng de dōng xi néng zì jǐ zhào guǎn zhěng lǐ me
（13）我所用的东西，能自己照管、整理么？

Can I take care of and organize my belongings?

wǒ de qián néng yòng dé qí dàng jì bù làng fèi yě bù lìn sè me
（14）我的钱，能用得其当，既不浪费，也不吝啬么？

Can I use my money wisely, neither wasting nor being stingy?

wǒ duì yú wǒ suǒ yīng zuò de gōng zuò néng fù zé qù zuò zuò shí qiě hěn yǒu xìng qù me
（15）我对于我所应做的工作，能负责去做，做时且很有兴趣么？

Can I take responsibility for my work and find joy in doing it?

wǒ duì yú gōng zuò hào fèi ruò gān jīng lì hào fèi ruò gān shí jiān néng tuǒ wéi zhī pèi me
（16）我对于工作，耗费若干精力，耗费若干时间，能妥为支配么？

Can I properly manage the energy and time I spend on work?

zhōng huá zhí yè xué xiào shǐ liào zhào piān
13）中华职业学校史料照片

Historical Photos of Zhonghua Vocational School

zhōng huá zhí yè jiào yù shè zài shàng hǎi chuàng bàn zhōng huá zhí yè xué xiào yǐ zuò shì fàn
中华职业教育社在上海创办中华职业学校以作示范，
xuǎn zhǐ zài pín mín qū lù jiā bāng shī shēng gòng tóng láo dòng zài yī piàn huāng dì shàng jiàn qǐ
选址在贫民区陆家浜，师生共同劳动，在一片荒地上建起
le xiào yuán
了校园。

The CVEA established Zhonghua Vocational School in Shanghai as a model, choosing a location in the working – class district of Lujiabang. Teachers and students worked together to build the campus on a piece of wasteland.

tú zhōng huá zhí yè xué xiào lù jiā bāng xiào zhǐ
图3－14 中华职业学校陆家浜校址

Fig. 3－14 Lujiabang campus of Zhonghua Vocational School

tú zhōng huá zhí yè xué xiào xiào shè
图3–15　中华职业学校校舍

Fig. 3 – 15　School buildings of Zhonghua Vocational School

tú zǎo nián céng jiù dú yú zhōng huá zhí yè xué xiào de zhù míng shù xué jiā huà luó gēng
图3–16 早年曾就读于中华职业学校的著名数学家华罗庚

Fig. 3 – 16 The renowned mathematician Hua Luogeng, who once studied at Zhonghua Vocational School

tú zhōng huá zhí yè xué xiào xué shēng zǎo cāo
图3–17 中华职业学校学生早操

Fig. 3 – 17 Students of Zhonghua Vocational School are doing morning exercises

tú zhōng huá zhí yè xué xiào yùn dòng huì kāi mù shì
图3–18 中华职业学校运动会开幕式

Fig. 3 – 18 The opening ceremony of a sports meet in Zhonghua Vocational School

tú zhōng huá zhí yè xué xiào lán qiú bǐ sài
图3–19　中华职业学校篮球比赛

Fig. 3 – 19　A basketball game in Zhonghua Vocational School

tú　zhōng huá zhí yè xué xiào kè jiān yóu xì
图3-20　中华职业学校课间游戏

Fig. 3-20　Students of Zhonghua Vocational School are playing during break time

tú　　zhōng huá zhí yè xué xiào yuè lǎn shì
图3-21　中华职业学校阅览室

Fig. 3 – 21　Reading room of Zhonghua Vocational School

tú zhōng huá zhí yè xué xiào zhū suàn jiào xué
图3-22 中华职业学校珠算教学

Fig. 3-22 Abacus classroom of Zhonghua Vocational School

tú zhōng huá zhí yè xué xiào dǎ zì kè
图3–23 中华职业学校打字课

Fig. 3 – 23 Typing class of Zhonghua Vocational School

tú zhōng huá zhí yè xué xiào fà láng kē shí zuò
图3-24 中华职业学校珐琅科实作

Fig. 3－24 Internship of the enamelware majors of Zhonghua Vocational School

tú zhōng huá zhí yè xué xiào jī xiè kē shí zuò
图 3–25 中华职业学校机械科实作

Fig. 3 – 25 Internship of the mechanical majors of Zhonghua Vocational School

tú zhōng huá zhí yè xué xiào tǔ mù kē shí zuò
图3-26 中华职业学校土木科实作

Fig. 3-26 Internship of the civil engineering majors of Zhonghua Vocational School

tú　　zhōng huá zhí yè xué xiào shāng kē shí zuò
图3－27　中华职业学校商科实作

Fig. 3－27　Internship of the business students of Zhonghua Vocational School

tú zhōng huá zhí yè xué xiào yín háng kuài jì shí zuò
图3–28 中华职业学校银行会计实作

Fig. 3 – 28 Internship of bank accounting majors of Zhonghua Vocational School

tú zhōng huá zhí yè xué xiào féng cì kē shí zuò
图3-29 中华职业学校缝刺科实作

Fig. 3 – 29 Internship of sewing and embroidery majors of Zhonghua Vocational School

tú zhōng huá zhí yè xué xiào cán sāng kē xué shēng xué xí yǎng cán
图3–30 中华职业学校蚕桑科学生学习养蚕

Fig. 3 – 30 Sericulture majors of Zhonghua Vocational School are learning how to raise silkworms

tú zhōng huá zhí yè xué xiào fù shǔ gōng chǎng chǎn pǐn
图3–31 中华职业学校附属工场产品1

Fig. 3 – 31 Product from the factory affiliated to Zhonghua Vocational School 1

图3-32　中华职业学校附属工场产品2

Fig. 3 - 32　Product from the factory affiliated to Zhonghua Vocational School 2

tú huáng yán péi xiān sheng shū fǎ
图3–33 黄炎培先生书法1

Fig. 3 – 33 Huang's calligraphy 1

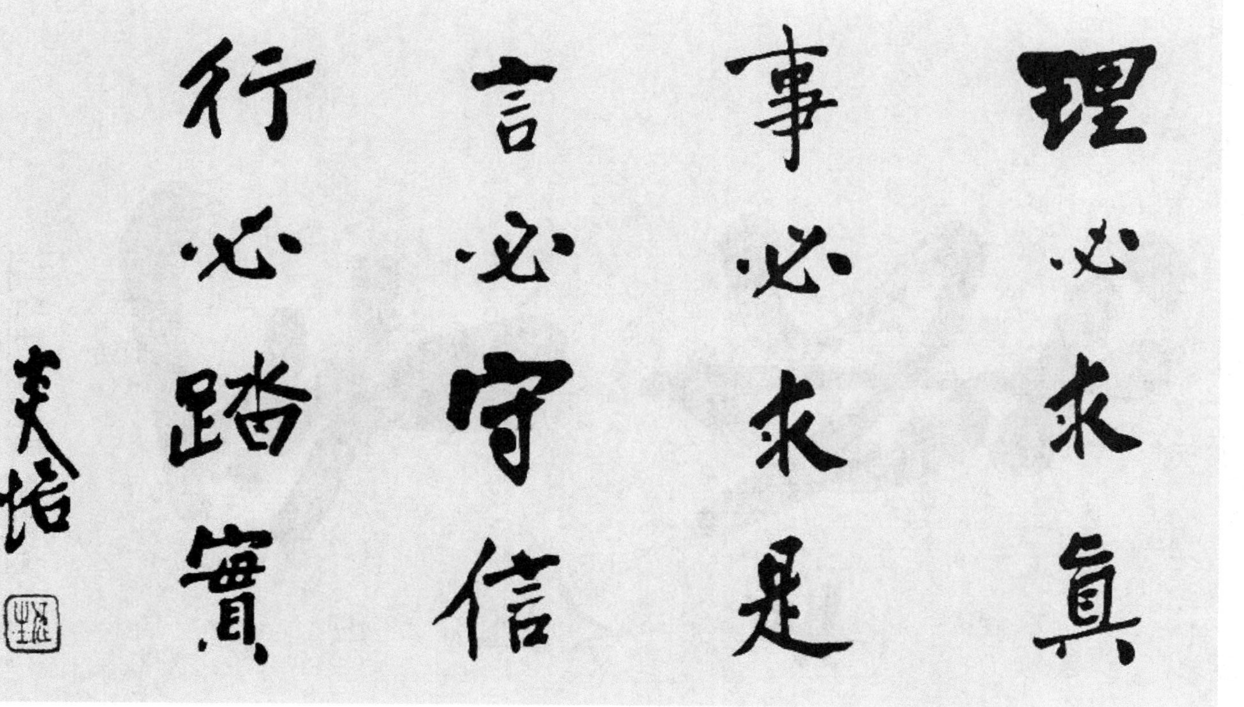

tú　huáng yán péi xiān sheng shū fǎ
图3–34　黄炎培先生书法2

Fig. 3 – 34　Huang's calligraphy 2

图3–35　黄炎培先生书法3

Fig. 3 – 35　Huang's calligraphy 3

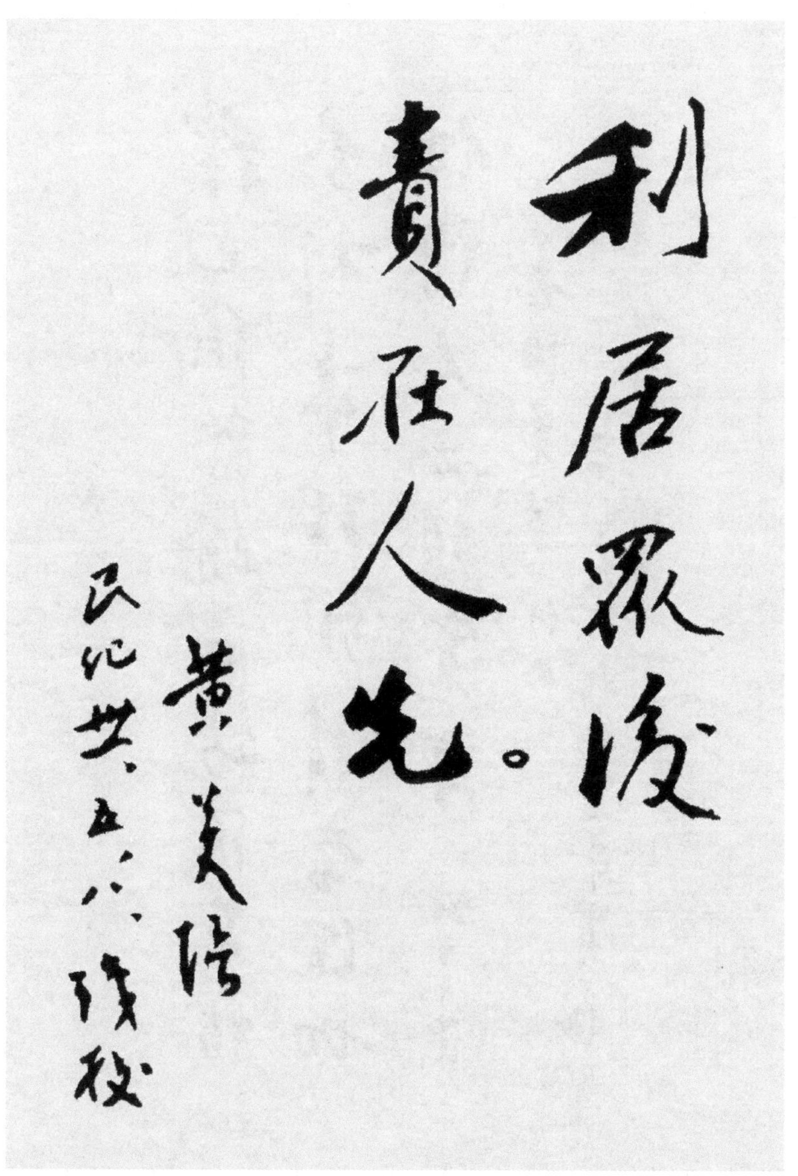

tú huáng yán péi xiān sheng shū fǎ
图3–36 黄炎培先生书法4

Fig. 3 – 36 Huang's calligraphy 4

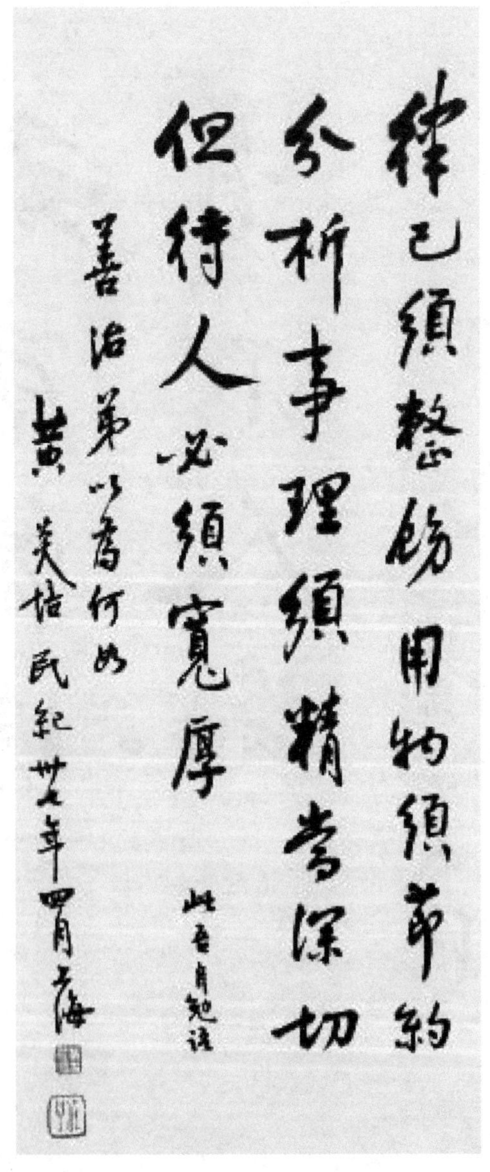

tú　　huáng yán péi xiān sheng shū fǎ
图3–37　黄炎培先生书法5

Fig. 3 – 37　Huang's calligraphy 5

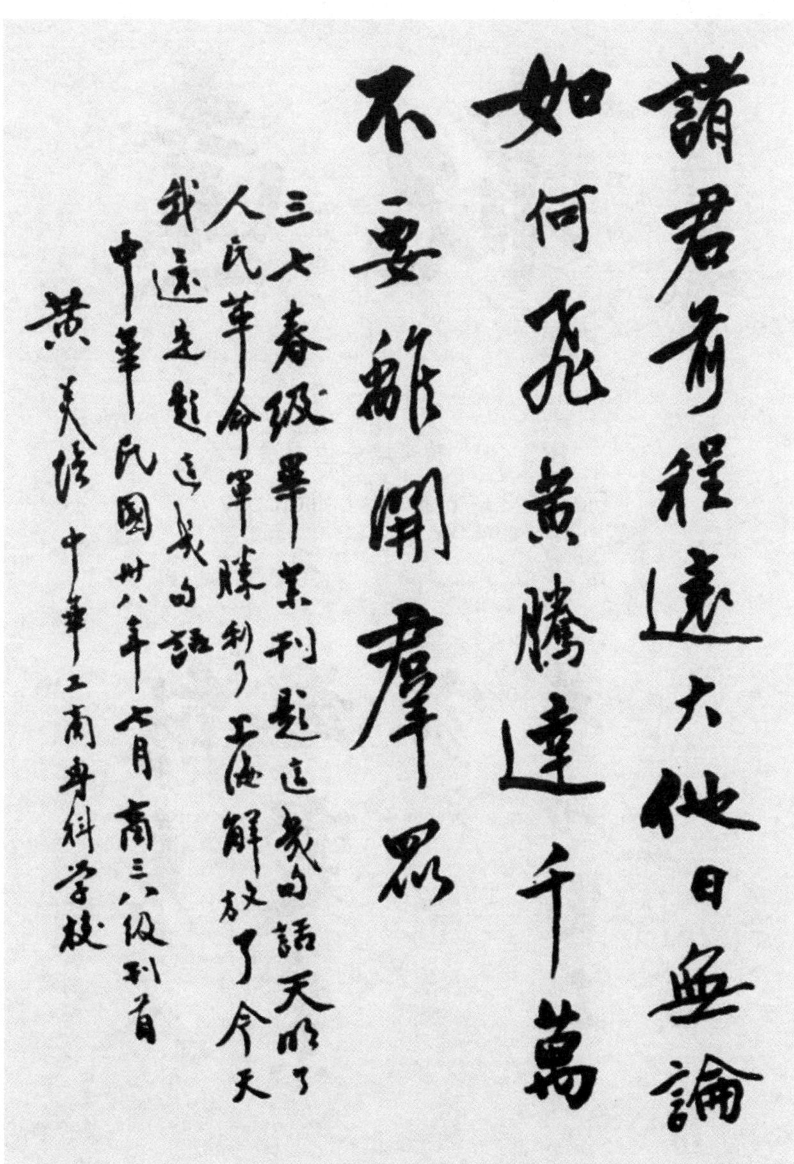

tú huáng yán péi xiān sheng shū fǎ
图3–38 黄炎培先生书法6

Fig. 3 – 38 Huang's calligraphy 6

tú huáng yán péi xiān sheng shū fǎ
图3–39 黄炎培先生书法7

Fig. 3 – 39 Huang's calligraphy 7

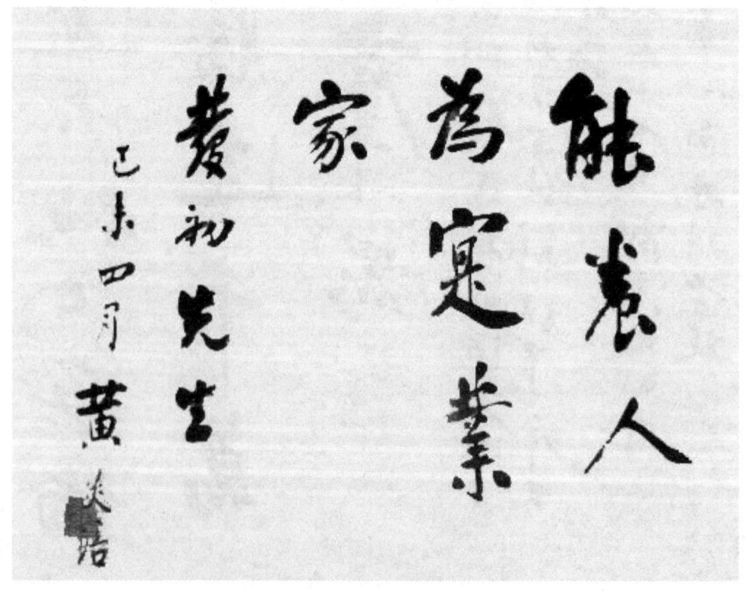

tú huáng yán péi xiān sheng shū fǎ
图3–40 黄炎培先生书法8

Fig. 3 – 40 Huang's calligraphy 8

参考文献 References

[1] 张杨群．立业立人：校园文化理念解读[M]．重庆：西南师范大学出版社，2013．

[2] 周汉民．敬业乐群·黄炎培职业教育思想读本：教师篇[M]．上海：上海科学技术文献出版社，2014．

[3] 周汉民．双手万能·黄炎培职业教育思想读本：学生篇[M]．上海：上海科学技术文献出版社，2014．

[4] 周汉民．理必求真·黄炎培职业教育思想读本：综合篇[M]．上海：上海科学技术文献出版社，2015．

[5] 黄炎培．职业教育论[M]．北京：商务印书馆，2019．

[6] 田正平，李笑贤. 黄炎培教育论著选[M]. 北京：人民教育出版社，2018.

[7] 中华职业教育社. 黄炎培教育文集[M]. 北京：中国文史出版社，2022.

cān kǎo wén xiàn

参考文献 References

[1] Zhang, Y. (2013). Establishing Careers and Cultivating Individuals: Interpretation of Campus Culture Concepts [M]. Chongqing: Southwest China Normal University Press.

[2] Zhou, H. (2014). Respecting One's Profession and Enjoying the Community: Huang Yanpei's Thoughts on Vocational Education (Teachers' Edition) [M]. Shanghai: Shanghai Scientific and Technical Literature Press.

[3] Zhou, H. (2014). Hands Wield Infinite Capability: Huang Yanpei's Thoughts on Vocational Education (Students' Edition) [M]. Shanghai: Shanghai Scientific and Technical Literature Press.

[4] Zhou, H. (2015). Pursuing Truth through Reasoning: Huang Yanpei's Thoughts on Vocational Education (Comprehensive Edition) [M]. Shanghai: Shanghai Scientific and Technical Literature Press.

[5] Huang, Y. (2019). On Vocational Education [M]. Beijing: The Commercial Press.

[6] Tian, Z., & Li, X. (2018). Selected Educational Works of Huang Yanpei [M]. Beijing: People's Education Press.

[7] National Association of Vocational Education of China. (2022). Collected Educational Works of Huang Yanpei [M]. Beijing: China Literature and History Press.